Miranda Remnek
Editor

Access to East European and Eurasian Culture: Publishing, Acquisitions, Digitization, Metadata

Access to East European and Eurasian Culture: Publishing, Acquisitions, Digitization, Metadata has been co-published simultaneously as *Slavic & East European Information Resources*, Volume 8, Numbers 2/3 2007.

Pre-publication REVIEWS, COMMENTARIES, EVALUATIONS...

"Addresses various aspects of Slavic librarianship, not shying away from or glossing over complexity or intellectual depth. This is not a '101' course on Slavic librarianship... Provides useful information for seasoned librarians as well as for new ones... Serves as AN EXCELLENT COLLECTION DEVELOPMENT RESOURCE FOR CONTEMPORARY SLAVIC LIBRARIANS ... Provides Slavic librarians with broad and deep coverage of topics dealt with on a regular basis... Presents a profile of what Slavic librarians do, how the work is done and how it is being tailored to fit librarianship of the future."

Janet Crayne, MA, ABD, MA
Head,
Slavic and East European Division
University of Michigan Library

More pre-publication
REVIEWS, COMMENTARIES, EVALUATIONS . . .

"ESSENTIAL not only for the professional librarians and bibliographers who work with the East European and Eurasian Collections but also to the researchers and scholars who study these areas."

Tatjana Lorkovic, MA, MLS, BA
Curator
*Slavic, East European
and Central Asian Collections
Yale University Library*

"A window into the world of contemporary Slavic Studies librarianship. . . . OFFERS A CLEAR PICTURE OF CURRENT AND DEVELOPING CHALLENGES throughout the lifecycle of academic collection, and research. From publication to acquisition, description and access, the text weaves and stitches a variety of perspectives—historical context, statistical assessment, and practical experience—to provide for the reader a broad understanding of the changing nature of the profession and how it is practiced."

James T. Simon
*Director of International Resources
Center for Research Libraries*

"Wide-ranging . . . offers A USEFUL SURVEY OF THE LATEST DEVELOPMENTS in the field of Slavic, Eurasian, and East European librarianship. . . . A fine job of bringing together the disparate contributions of the participants into a useful whole, whose sum is greater than its parts. . . . Manages to capture the exciting diversity of approaches to some of the most important issues in Slavic librarianship today. . . . A welcome addition to the literature . . . will no doubt inspire and serve as a model for future collaborative digital projects. . . . BELONGS ON THE WORKING BOOKSHELF OF EVERY SLAVIC LIBRARIAN."

Ernest A. Zitser, PhD
*Librarian for Slavic
and East European Studies
& Adjunct Assistant Professor
Dept. of Slavic and Eurasian Studies
Duke University*

More pre-publication
REVIEWS, COMMENTARIES, EVALUATIONS . . .

"This diverse collection of articles represents A TIMELY AND WELCOME CONTRIBUTION to the evolving field of Eastern European and Eurasian librarianship. . . a useful snapshot of the current state of the field, and would be a GREAT ADDITION TO ACADEMIC LIBRARY COLLECTIONS dedicated to Eastern European, Slavic and Eurasian materials."

Anna L. Shparberg
Librarian for History, German and Slavic studies, Fondren Library Rice University, Houston

"A SENSIBLY SELECTED COLLECTION of articles that, presented together in one place, illustrate, most of all, the truly dynamic nature of contemporary Slavic librarianship. It not only provides a well-organized tour around the bustling frontier of the field, that is, digitization, but also revisits its traditional center, print culture. No need to mention that it SHOULD BE READ BY ALL PRACTICING SLAVIC LIBRARIANS and adopted as a required reading by all classes related to Slavic Bibliography. . . . DOES AN EXCELLENT JOB in showing us how the mega geopolitical changes of recent years combined with the rapid technological developments to reconfigure—if not redefine—the field of Slavic librarianship as one with new opportunities and challenges, and how the Slavic librarians have been dealing with those. Of particular interests are those articles describing current digitization projects. The inclusion of foreign experiences (of Ukrainian and Bulgarian libraries) in it is another positive feature of this book given the relative paucity of literature in English in that area."

Wook-Jin Cheun, MA, MLS
*Librarian
for Slavic and East European Studies
Indiana University Libraries
Bloomington, Indiana*

Access to East European and Eurasian Culture: Publishing, Acquisitions, Digitization, Metadata

Access to East European and Eurasian Culture: Publishing, Acquisitions, Digitization, Metadata has been co-published simultaneously as *Slavic & East European Information Resources*, Volume 8, Numbers 2/3 2007.

> **Monographic Separates from** *Slavic & East European Information Resources*™
>
> For additional information on these and other Haworth Press titles, including descriptions, tables of contents, reviews, and prices, use the QuickSearch catalog at http://www.HaworthPress.com.

Access to East European and Eurasian Culture: Publishing, Acquisitions, Digitization, Metadata, edited by Miranda Remnek, PhD, MA, MLS (Vol. 8, No. 2/3, 2007). *A collection of superb presentations from a 2006 conference on* Book Arts, Culture, and Media in Russia, East Europe and Eurasia: From Print to Digital *that describes access challenges and advances in publishing, acquisitions, digitization, and metadata.*

Tracking a Diaspora: Émigrés from Russia and Eastern Europe in the Repositories, edited by Anatol Shmelev, PhD (Vol. 7, No. 2/3, 2006). *Examination of little-known and underutilized information resources about the history of emigration from Russia and the USSR.*

Virtual Slavica: Digital Libraries, Digital Archives, edited by Michael Neubert, MLS, MAIS (Vol. 6, No. 2/3, 2005). *An examination of the most significant aspects of presenting Slavic studies materials via the Internet in libraries and archives, including copyright issues, digital references, and text encoding.*

A Guide to Slavic Collections in the United States and Canada, edited by Allan Urbanic, PhD, and Beth Feinberg, MS (Vol. 5, No. 3/4, 2004). *A directory of libraries with collections of Slavic materials; provides general information about each library, specifics about its collections and electronic resources, and contact information.*

Russian and East European Books and Manuscripts in the United States: Proceedings of a Conference in Honor of the Fiftieth Anniversary of the Bakhmeteff Archive of Russian and East European History and Culture, edited by Tanya Chebotarev and Jared S. Ingersoll (Vol. 4, No. 4, 2003). *This book documents the concerted effort to preserve Russian and East European written culture outside the bounds of Communist power.*

Judaica in the Slavic Realm, Slavica in the Judaic Realm: Repositories, Collections, Projects, Publications, edited by Zachary M. Baker, MA (Vol. 4, No. 2/3, 2003). *A collection of essays, bibliographies, and research studies illustrating the state of Jewish-related publishing ventures in Eastern Europe and the former Soviet Union, and documenting efforts by Judaic scholars, librarians, and genealogists to provide access to archival collections in those countries.*

Libraries in Open Societies: Proceedings of the Fifth International Slavic Librarians' Conference, edited by Harold M. Leich, MLS (Vol. 3, No. 2/3, 2002). *"The papers collected in this book are not only the product of this international conference, but also are concrete evidence of how far Slavic librarianship has progressed over the past 30 years. Valuable–not only to those with an interest in the Slavic field but to any librarian with an interest in area studies librarianship, international networking, and collection development." (Robert H. Burger, PhD, MLS, former Head of the Slavic and East European Library, University of Illinois at Urbana-Champaign)*

Publishing in Yugoslavia's Successor States, edited by Michael Biggins, PhD, MS, and Janet Crayne, MLIS, MA (Vol. 1, No. 2/3, 2000). *"A valuable tool, one which has been sorely lacking. All regions of the area are covered. The list of vendors, most with contact information that includes Web sites, will certainly be of service to those charged with acquiring these publications. An indispensible resource for anyone needing access to the publications of this region." (Allan Urbanic, PhD, MLIS, Librarian for Slavic Collections, University of California, Berkeley)*

Access to East European and Eurasian Culture: Publishing, Acquisitions, Digitization, Metadata

Miranda Remnek, PhD, MA, MLS
Editor

Access to East European and Eurasian Culture: Publishing, Acquisitions, Digitization, Metadata has been co-published simultaneously as *Slavic & East European Information Resources*, Volume 8, Numbers 2/3 2007.

The Haworth Information Press®
An Imprint of The Haworth Press, Inc.

New York • London • Victoria (AU)
www.HaworthPress.com

Published by

The Haworth Information Press®, 10 Alice Street, Binghamton, NY 13904-1580 USA

The Haworth Information Press® is an imprint of The Haworth Press, Inc., 10 Alice Street, Binghamton, NY 13904-1580 USA.

Access to East European and Eurasian Culture: Publishing, Acquisitions, Digitization, Metadata has been co-published simultaneously as *Slavic & East European Information Resources*, Volume 8, Numbers 2/3 2007.

© 2007 by The Haworth Press, Inc. All rights reserved. No part of this work may be reproduced or utilized in any form or by any means, electronic or mechanical, including photocopying, microfilm and recording, or by any information storage and retrieval system, without permission in writing from the publisher. Printed in the United States of America.

The development, preparation, and publication of this work has been undertaken with great care. However, the publisher, employees, editors, and agents of The Haworth Press and all imprints of The Haworth Press, Inc., including The Haworth Medical Press® and Pharmaceutical Products Press®, are not responsible for any errors contained herein or for consequences that may ensue from use of materials or information contained in this work. With regard to case studies, identities and circumstances of individuals discussed herein have been changed to protect confidentiality. Any resemblance to actual persons, living or dead, is entirely coincidental.

The Haworth Press is committed to the dissemination of ideas and information according to the highest standards of intellectual freedom and the free exchange of ideas. Statements made and opinions expressed in this publication do not necessarily reflect the views of the Publisher, Directors, management, or staff of The Haworth Press, Inc. or an endorsement by them.

Library of Congress Cataloging-in-Publication Data

Access to East European and Eurasian culture : publishing, acquisitions, digitization, metadata / Miranda Remnek, editor.
    p. cm.
"Co-published simultaneously as Slavic & East European information resources , volume 8, numbers 2/3 2007."
Includes bibliographical references and index.
ISBN 978-0-7890-3395-6 (alk. paper) – ISBN 978-0-7890-3396-3 (pbk. : alk. paper)
    1. Libraries–Special collections–Slavic countries. 2. Libraries–Special collections–Europe, Eastern. 3. Slavic countries–Digital libraries. 4. Europe, Eastern–Digital libraries. I. Remnek, Miranda Beaven. II. Slavic & East European information resources.
Z688.S56A65 2007
025.00285–dc22

    2007026939

The HAWORTH PRESS Inc.
Abstracting, Indexing & Outward Linking
PRINT and ELECTRONIC BOOKS & JOURNALS

This section provides you with a list of major indexing & abstracting services and other tools for bibliographic access. That is to say, each service began covering this periodical during the year noted in the right column. Most Websites which are listed below have indicated that they will either post, disseminate, compile, archive, cite or alert their own Website users with research-based content from this work. (This list is as current as the copyright date of this publication.)

Abstracting, Website/Indexing Coverage . . . . Year When Coverage Began

- *Academic Search Premier (EBSCO)*
  <http://www.search.ebscohost.com> 2006
- *Academic Source Premier (EBSCO)* <http://search.ebscohost.com> . . 2007
- *American Bibliography of Slavic and East European Studies (ABSEES & ABSEES Online)*
  <http://www.library.uiuc.edu/absees/> 2000
- *British Library Inside (The British Library)*
  <http://www.bl.uk/services/current/inside.html> 2007
- *Cambridge Scientific Abstracts (now ProQuest CSA)*
  <http://www.csa.com> 2006
- *Computer & Control Abstracts (INSPEC–The Institution of Engineering and Technology)* <http://www.iee.org.uk/publish/> . . . 2006
- *Current Abstracts (EBSCO)* <http://search.ebscohost.com> 2007
- *Current Citations Express (EBSCO)* <http://search.ebscohost.com> . . . 2007
- *EBSCOhost Electronic Journals Service (EJS)*
  <http://search.ebscohost.com> 2001
- *Electrical & Electronics Abstracts (INSPEC–The Institution of Engineering and Technology)*
  <http://www.iee.org.uk/publish/> 2006
- *Electronic Collections Online (OCLC)*
  <http://www.oclc.org/electroniccollections> 2006
- *Elsevier Eflow-D* <http://www.elsevier.com> 2006
- *Elsevier Scopus* <http://www.info.scopus.com> 2005
- *Google* <http://www.google.com> 2004

(continued)

- *Google Scholar* <http://scholar.google.com> 2004
- *Haworth Document Delivery Center*
  <http://www.HaworthPress.com/journals/dds.asp> 2000
- *Imaging Abstracts* <http://www.intertechpira.com>.............. 2007
- *Index Copernicus* <http://www.indexcopernicus.com> 2006
- *Informed Librarian, The* <http://www.informedlibrarian.com> 2003
- *INSPEC (The Institution of Engineering and Technology)*
  <http://www.iee.org.uk/publish/>........................... 2002
- *International Bibliography of Book Reviews
  on the Humanities and Social Sciences (IBR) (Thomson)*
  <http://www.saur.de> 2006
- *International Bibliography of Periodical Literature
  on the Humanities and Social Sciences (IBZ) (Thomson)*
  <http://www.saur.de> 2000
- *Internationale Bibliographie der geistes- und
  sozialwissenschaftlichen Zeitschriftenliteratur ... See IBZ*
  <http://www.saur.de> 2000
- *JournalSeek* <http://www.journalseek.net> 2006
- *Konyvtari Figyelo (Library Review)*
  <http://www.oszk.hu/index_en.htm> 2000
- *Library, Information Science & Technology Abstracts (EBSCO)*
  <http://www.search.ebscohost.com> 2006
- *Library, Information Science & Technology Abstracts (EBSCO)*
  <http://search.ebscohost.com>............................. 2007
- *Links@Ovid (via CrossRef targeted DOI links)*
  <http://www.ovid.com>..................................... 2005
- *LISA: Library and Information Science Abstracts (ProQuest CSA)*
  <http://www.csa.com/factsheets/list-set-c.php>.................... 2006
- *Management & Marketing Abstracts*
  <http://www.intertechpira.com/> 2000
- *MasterFILE Premier (EBSCO)*
  <http://www.search.ebscohost.com> 2006
- *NewJour (Electronic Journals & Newsletters)*
  <http://gort.ucsd.edu/newjour/>........................... 2006
- *OCLC ArticleFirst* <http://www.oclc.org/services/databases/> 2006
- *Ovid Linksolver (Open URL link resolver via CrossRef
  targeted DOI links)* <http://www.linksolver.com> 2005
- *Packaging Month* <http:www.intertechpira.com> 2007
- *Paperbase Abstracts* <http://www.intertechpira.com> 2007
- *Physics Abstracts (INSPEC–The Institution of Engineering
  and Technology)* <http://www.iee.org.uk/publish/>............. 2006

(continued)

- *Press <http://www.intertechpira.com>* 2000
- *Public Affairs Information Service (PAIS) International (ProQuest CSA) <http://www.pais.org/www.csa.com>* 2000
- *Referativnyi Zhurnal (Abstracts Journal of the All-Russian Institute of Scientific and Technical Information– in Russian) <http://www.viniti.ru>* 2000
- *Scopus (see instead Elsevier Scopus) <http://www.info.scopus.com>* 2005
- *Subject Index to Literature on Electronic Sources of Information <http://library.usask.ca/~dworacze/BIBLIO.HTM>* 2000
- *TOC Premier (EBSCO) <http://search.ebscohost.com>* 2007
- *zetoc (The British Library) <http://www.bl.uk>* 2007

Bibliographic Access

- *Cabell's Directory of Publishing Opportunities in Educational Technology & Library Science <http://www.cabells.com>*
- *Magazines for Libraries (Katz)*
- *MediaFinder <http://www.mediafinder.com/>*
- *Ulrich's Periodicals Directory: International Periodicals Information Since 1932 <http://www.Bowkerlink.com>*

Special Bibliographic Notes related to special journal issues (separates) and indexing/abstracting:

- indexing/abstracting services in this list will also cover material in any "separate" that is co-published simultaneously with Haworth's special thematic journal issue or DocuSerial. Indexing/abstracting usually covers material at the article/chapter level.
- monographic co-editions are intended for either non-subscribers or libraries which intend to purchase a second copy for their circulating collections.
- monographic co-editions are reported to all jobbers/wholesalers/approval plans. The source journal is listed as the "series" to assist the prevention of duplicate purchasing in the same manner utilized for books-in-series.
- to facilitate user/access services all indexing/abstracting services are encouraged to utilize the co-indexing entry note indicated at the bottom of the first page of each article/chapter/contribution.
- this is intended to assist a library user of any reference tool (whether print, electronic, online, or CD-ROM) to locate the monographic version if the library has purchased this version but not a subscription to the source journal.
- individual articles/chapters in any Haworth publication are also available through the Haworth Document Delivery Service (HDDS).

As part of Haworth's continuing commitment to better serve our library patrons, we are proud to be working with the following electronic services:

AGGREGATOR SERVICES

EBSCOhost

Ingenta

J-Gate

Minerva

OCLC FirstSearch

Oxmill

SwetsWise

LINK RESOLVER SERVICES

1Cate (Openly Informatics)

ChemPort (American Chemical Society)

CrossRef

Gold Rush (Coalliance)

LinkOut (PubMed)

LINKplus (Atypon)

LinkSolver (Ovid)

LinkSource with A-to-Z (EBSCO)

Resource Linker (Ulrich)

SerialsSolutions (ProQuest)

SFX (Ex Libris)

Sirsi Resolver (SirsiDynix)

Tour (TDnet)

Vlink (Extensity, formerly Geac)

WebBridge (Innovative Interfaces)

Access to East European and Eurasian Culture: Publishing, Acquisitions, Digitization, Metadata

CONTENTS

Foreword   xiii
    Bradley L. Schaffner

Guest Editor's Introduction   1
    Miranda Remnek

PUBLISHING

The Diversification of Russian Scholarly Publishing, 1995-2005   7
    John Bushnell

The Slovak Periodical Press: Historical Development, Current Content, New Forms of Access   21
    Peter Olekšák
    Albert Kulla

ACQUISITIONS

Iltimos, bizga kitoblar yuboring! U.S. Libraries' Collecting Strategies for Central Asian Publications   31
    Karen Rondestvedt

Modern Greek Collections at U.S. Libraries: New Directions   49
    Harold M. Leich

Acquisitions Problems in Ukrainian Libraries and New Electronic Solutions   55
    Olena Bashun

DIGITIZATION

The Methodological Advantages of Digital Editions:
   The Case of Eighteenth-Century Russian Texts   71
      Marcus C. Levitt

Internet Resources on Russian History: The Electronic Library
   at Moscow State University   85
      Leonid Borodkin
      Timur Valetov

Russia Beyond Russia Digital Library:
   History, Concept, and Development   95
      Nadia Zilper
      Rita Van Duinen

Implementing an Image Database for Complex Russian
   Architectural Objects: The William Brumfield Collection   109
      James D. West
      Eileen Llona
      Theodore Gerontakos
      Michael Biggins

Digitizing the Zdenka and Stanley B. Winters Collection
   of Czech and Slovak Posters, 1920-1991   127
      Patricia Hswe

METADATA

Application of MARC21–Concise Format for Bibliographic
   Data in Bulgarian Libraries: The Case of the Central Library
   of the Bulgarian Academy of Sciences   137
      Sabina Aneva

The Librarian's Role in Promoting Digital Scholarship:
   Development and Metadata Issues   151
      Eileen Llona

Index   165

ABOUT THE EDITOR

Miranda Remnek, PhD, MA, MLS, is Head, Slavic & East European Library, University of Illinois at Urbana-Champaign. She currently serves as chair of the Bibliography & Documentation Committee of the American Association for the Advancement of Slavic Studies, and as co-chair of its Digital Projects Subcommittee. Dr. Remnek's interests since the mid-1990s have included the production of scholarly electronic texts in the humanities. Besides her responsibilities for the East European collections at the University of Minnesota from 1979 to 2002, she also assumed coordination of its Electronic Text Research Center in 1996. This involved the founding of several digital humanities projects including *Early 19th-century Russian Readership* and *Culture, and UVSOTA: Undergraduate Victorian Studies Online Teaching Anthology*. Since moving to Illinois she has published several articles on technology in Slavic studies, and has also initiated a number of related digital initiatives: an annual Slavic Digital Text Workshop, a AAASS-sponsored *Inventory of Slavic, East European and Eurasian Digital Projects*, and an educational wiki for Slavic scholars and librarians entitled *Digital Slavist*.

Dr. Remnek also has a long-standing interest in Russian book studies and has numerous publications in the field, beginning with a series of articles in the mid-1980s on publishing in early 19th-century Russia. She later edited *Books in Russia and the Soviet Union: Past and Present* (Wiesbaden: Harrassowitz, 1991). In 1999 she was awarded the PhD in Late Modern European History at UC Berkeley for a quantitative study of middle-class reading in Russia entitled "The Expansion of Russian Reading Audiences, 1828-1848." Her later articles based on this research have appeared in collections published by Duke UP in 2001 and Cambridge UP in 2002. Dr. Remnek's most recent print culture interests include merchant reading practices in Russia and Siberia in the 19th century. She is currently editing a group of articles delivered at a conference she organized at Illinois in June 2006; the collection is entitled *The Space of the Book in Russia's Social Imagination*.

∞ ALL HAWORTH INFORMATION PRESS BOOKS AND JOURNALS ARE PRINTED ON CERTIFIED ACID-FREE PAPER

Foreword

The past two decades witnessed the collapse of the Soviet Union and the demise of communist-led governments in East Central Europe. Along with great political and economic upheavals that come with such revolutions, there were substantial changes to the scholarly publishing industry of these countries. During this period, regional publishing and distribution systems fell into a state of turmoil, making it extremely difficult for Slavic librarians to identify and acquire books and journals or even to provide access to information.

Simultaneously with the chaos in the Slavic and Eurasian publishing industry, another revolution was occuring in academic and research libraries in the form of an "IT" explosion. Formats for scholarly communication were quickly evolving to take advantage of new computing and web-based technologies. Not only did Slavic librarians have to scramble to develop new approaches to successfully fulfill their primary professional responsibilities of developing Slavic and Eurasian collections, but they also had to deal with the changing nature of scholarly publishing itself. Practitioners had to develop new ways to acquire and assess the myriad of materials emanating from East Central Europe and the Soviet successor states, while at the same time they also had to develop new skills and approaches to academic librarianship in general.

Given the recent turmoil of the publishing industry in Slavic and Eurasian regions, no one could blame any librarian for simply focusing his or her efforts on acquiring materials from the area and ignoring all of the changes taking place in regard to scholarly communication, particularly in the realm of digital publishing. The essays published in the present volume demonstrate that Slavic librarians, far from ignoring change,

---

Bradley L. Schaffner holds an MA and MLS from Indiana University, Bloomington and is Head of the Slavic Division of Widener Library of Harvard College Library, Harvard University, Cambridge, MA 02138 (E-mail: bschaffn@fas.harvard.edu).

[Haworth co-indexing entry note]: "Foreword." Schaffner, Bradley L. Co-published simultaneously in *Slavic & East European Information Resources* (The Haworth Information Press, an imprint of The Haworth Press, Inc.) Vol. 8, No. 2/3, 2007, pp. xxi-xxii; and: *Access to East European and Eurasian Culture: Publishing, Acquisitions, Digitization, Metadata* (ed: Miranda Remnek) The Haworth Information Press, an imprint of The Haworth Press, Inc., 2007, pp.xiii-xiv. Single or multiple copies of this article are available for a fee from The Haworth Document Delivery Service [1-800-HAWORTH, 9:00 a.m. - 5:00 p.m. (EST). E-mail address: docdelivery@haworthpress.com].

Available online at http://seeir.haworthpress.com
© 2007 by The Haworth Press, Inc. All rights reserved.

have embraced new technologies that are impacting scholarly communication. The volume further illustrates that during this period of publishing disorder, Slavic librarians have learned to value and embrace flexibility, openness to new ideas, and the power of imagination in dealing with these changes.

The contributions published in this book represent an international partnership of both librarians and scholars in the fields of Slavic and Eurasian studies. Several of these essays discuss projects that clearly demonstrate the increasing collaboration between the two groups as new scholarly communication technologies are developed and refined. Five essays included in this work focus on publishing and the acquisition of materials from this area of the world. These articles indicate that the publishing industries of the region have recovered from the turmoil of the late 1980s and early 1990s, and are once again functioning to varying degrees of success. In addition, librarians are finding ways to acquire these materials in a timely and cost-effective manner. Seven commentaries deal with utilizing new technologies to create resources and to improve access to Slavic and Eurasian materials. The pieces on the Brumfield Russian architectural photograph collection at the University of Washington, the digitization of twentieth-century Czech and Slovak posters at the University of Illinois, and the creation of digital access to the André Savine Collection at the University of North Carolina, Chapel Hill, to name a few, illustrate that Slavic librarians are indeed successfully embracing new technologies to enhance access to scholarly information.

The papers published in this volume clearly demonstrate the important work that specialists in the field are accomplishing, not only to acquire Slavic and Eurasian publications, but also to make such material available through the employment of new technologies to create user-friendly resources allowing students and scholars from around the globe to access important research materials. This publication provides a welcome snapshot of the current condition of scholarly publishing and communication regarding Slavic and Eurasian resources.

Bradley L. Schaffner

Guest Editor's Introduction

Miranda Remnek

The papers in this volume were originally prepared for the 2006 Ralph and Ruth Fisher Forum and associated workshops held at the University of Illinois at Urbana-Champaign in June 2006. Four were presented at the 2006 Slavic Librarians' Workshop on June 15. The others were presented June 17-18 at the Forum itself, entitled "Book Arts, Culture and Media in Russia, Eastern Europe and Eurasia: From Print to Digital." Numerous topics were addressed, but the papers included here fall under the theme of *Access to East European and Eurasian Culture: Publishing, Acquisitions, Digitization, Metadata.*

PUBLISHING

The two papers in this category address a variety of concerns with regard to publishing in Russia and Eastern Europe. Given all that one hears about increasing tensions in the realm of the press in Russia, the first essay paints a contrary and welcome picture. In a thought-provoking overview of recent trends in scholarly publishing, John Bushnell

---

Miranda Remnek, PhD, MA, MLS, is Head, Slavic and East European Library and Professor of Library Administration, University of Illinois at Urbana-Champaign, 1408 West Gregory Drive, Urbana, IL 61801 USA (E-mail: mremnek@uiuc.edu).

Special thanks are due to *SEEIR* editor, Karen Rondestvedt, for editorial assistance with two of the essays in this collection.

[Haworth co-indexing entry note]: "Guest Editor's Introduction." Remnek, Miranda. Co-published simultaneously in *Slavic & East European Information Resources* (The Haworth Information Press, an imprint of The Haworth Press, Inc.) Vol. 8, No. 2/3, 2007, pp. 1-6; and: *Access to East European and Eurasian Culture: Publishing, Acquisitions, Digitization, Metadata* (ed: Miranda Remnek) The Haworth Information Press, an imprint of The Haworth Press, Inc., 2007, pp. 1-6. Single or multiple copies of this article are available for a fee from The Haworth Document Delivery Service [1-800-HAWORTH, 9:00 a.m. - 5:00 p.m. (EST). E-mail address: docdelivery@haworthpress.com].

Available online at http://seeir.haworthpress.com
© 2007 by The Haworth Press, Inc. All rights reserved.
doi:10.1300/J167v08n02_01

presents evidence to suggest that Russian output has not declined, but rather has doubled over the past ten years–and moreover that private publishers are leading this development. An informative essay that cogently summarizes and skillfully interprets the major characteristics of scholarly publishing (such as the fact that most collections of archival sources are issued not by archives but by private presses), Bushnell's detailed overview–especially his typology of commercial publishers with scholarly lists and his analysis of the sources that underpin much of Russian publishing–will be of interest to many librarians and scholars as they seek to navigate the new waters of post-Soviet Russian print culture.

Peter Olekšák and Albert Kulla present a broad overview of Slovak periodical publishing in the second half of the twentieth century to the present. Their main period of focus is from World War II, although their description of Slovak periodicals in the diaspora begins in the late nineteenth century. They emphasize the differences in content in recent years–especially after the Velvet Revolution of 1989–with new freedom for religious topics, and an emerging focus on family issues, women, advice, and entertainment. They note that new titles are emerging regularly, as well as new forms of online access for both large dailies and titles with lesser circulation. Although the digitization of Slovak books and serials is still somewhat in its infancy, university libraries have been providing access to student theses and their own publications in PDF format for the last six years. In addition, a major scanning effort of 350,000 volumes at the Slovak National Library is scheduled to begin in December 2008.

ACQUISITIONS

A second group of three papers deals with current acquisitions practices and possibilities for three distinct areas–Central Asia, Greece, and Ukraine–which traditionally were somewhat underrepresented in U.S. Slavic collections, but which now, owing to new geopolitical realities, are attracting considerably more attention. Central Asia is an increasingly important focus of attention, and yet U.S. libraries frequently express dissatisfaction with the volume of Central Asian receipts. But in her detailed study of collecting strategies employed by U.S. libraries to obtain good coverage of Central Asian publications, Karen Rondestvedt (Stanford University) presents evidence to suggest that their relatively small numbers are simply reflective of limited publishing output. In his overview of Modern Greek acquisitions in U.S. libraries and recent efforts to expand them, Harold Leich (Library of Congress) points out that although Greece "is something of an orphaned country when it comes to how American libraries traditionally divide the world," in recent years librarians have developed a number of innovative approaches to help improve access to that country's publishing output. Finally, Olena Bashun presents an overview of current acquisition challenges facing libraries in Ukraine as they seek to develop their traditional print collections, and also to implement access to a range of publications available in electronic form. She underscores the fact that there is now no reliable guide to Ukrainian books in print, which complicates the situation for both domestic colleagues and librarians abroad. As regards e-publications, she notes that besides purchasing access to ready-made databases, Ukrainian libraries are indeed creating their own full-text databases–especially at the National Library, and especially in regard to science texts, literary classics, rare books, reference and legal materials, and (as in the case of Slovakia) doctoral dissertations.

DIGITIZATION

The next five papers deal with various digital themes. The first two by Marcus Levitt and Leonid Borodkin (professors of Slavic Languages & Literatures and History respectively) focus largely on digital texts. In a wide-ranging paper that departs from the practical bent of most papers in this collection and also lays out a partial typology of digital texts (critical edition, text library, or web archive), Marcus Levitt presents the theoretical perspective of a scholar already highly receptive to the potential offered by digital technology for the creation of *critical editions*. But whether viewed as a means of producing a micro-level critical edition, or a macro-level corpus, Levitt explains the potential of this technology in terms of "the . . . new analytical methods that are possible"–an enormously important consideration for emerging digital scholars. He also defines the methodological advantages of digital technology in a manner close to the heart of working librarians: as a "quantum leap in making critical editions more effective information-managing tools." But he is careful to describe the challenging differences between critical editions (often more "accessible" or "optimized"), and documentary editions (more "archaeological" or "authentic," especially when they concern earlier time periods)–and exemplifies them in regard to eighteenth-century Russian texts. He first implies that these problems apply to digital as well as print editions, but then suggests that digital editions obviate the need to make choices. One may say that the digital solution is not so simple, but these are highly interesting issues for scholarly producers–and for the librarians assisting them.

The next piece, a report by Leonid Borodkin and Timur Valetov about Internet resources on Russian history at Moscow State University (MGU), exemplifies the *text library* model articulated by Levitt. The Electronic Library of the Faculty of History at MGU holds a substantial number of online texts that relate to different periods of global history. It contains about 100 texts on Russian history electronically published within the MGU project, as well as links to hundreds of other historical sources on Russian history on the Internet. Project texts are usually accompanied by short annotations with comments on the role of the document in Russian history. Another important component of the Electronic Library is an example of a topic-oriented historical Internet-resource (TOHIR) on Russian/Soviet labor history. Online access to the catalog of resources within the TOHIR is provided on the basis of MySQL and PHP-scripts.

The following paper, by Nadia Zilper and Rita Van Duinen on the *Russia Beyond Russia* Digital Library, essentially exemplifies the third model articulated by Levitt, a *web archive* of disparate digitized resources including digital texts. In their article the authors discuss their experience in building the *Russia Beyond Russia* Digital Library (RBR) funded by the Andrew W. Mellon Foundation. The basis of the RBR is the André Savine Collection at the University of North Carolina (UNC) containing over 60,000 items and archives of 30,000 pages (printed books, journals, periodicals; hand- and type-written newspapers, journals, books and other manuscripts; photographs, postcards, sound recordings, and currency). The authors trace the evolution of the RBR, and describe its conceptual model. Its key idea is to unite the different parts of the collection through indexing, and this is achieved by creating a modular digital library with a central scalable index hub called the Core Module. Special emphasis has been placed on resource discovery. Each UNC OPAC record for materials in the RBR will provide users with a direct link to the Core Module database via a stable URL. UNC OPAC records are available in WorldCat; thus users of WorldCat will have access to the RBR Core Module.

The last two papers in this group deal with the digitization of graphic culture. In a team-authored paper on the Brumfield architecture collection, Michael Biggins and his colleagues at the University of

Washington describe an ambitious, inter-institutional, scholar-librarian collaboration that seeks to apply appropriate digital technology to the preservation and dissemination of a substantial number of graphic images of a host of Russian architectural monuments. A corpus that in its totality numbers approximately 100,000 photographs, the William Brumfield collection has been assembled over the course of many years and now represents a unique resource that is insufficiently utilized and in great danger of irreversible deterioration (many slides are now twenty to thirty years old). The project team is applying the latest standards to the digitization and presentation of this remarkable collection, and, as with the RBR project, the care and sophistication with which Brumfield project routines were developed should serve as a model to all who set out to pursue a similar effort of this magnitude.

Finally, Patricia Hswe–in an account of a smaller graphic conversion project–describes the development and management issues encountered in digitizing the Stanley B. Winters collection of twentieth-century Czech and Slovak posters at the University of Illinois. The essay provides a nice counterbalance to the much more ambitious requirements and challenges of a project as significant as the Brumfield project, and in so doing perhaps stays closer to the demands more frequently encountered as librarians collaborate with faculty to provide new access to small pockets of research materials.

METADATA

Finally, two papers deal with issues in the realm of metadata, with reference to Slavic materials. In her paper on the use of MARC21 in Bulgarian libraries, Sabina Aneva shows how the Central Library of the Bulgarian Academy of Sciences (BASCL) created templates that accommodate traditional cataloging and the specificities of Bulgarian publishing. It has also created a MARC21 e-Club that allows major Bulgarian libraries to pool their expertise as they move to an electronic interchange environment. BASCL already uses ALEPH5000 with MARC21, and with the implementation of version 16, they will set up an X-Server to export bibliographic data in MARC XML format. Related to this is a striking collaboration between BASCL librarians and Slavic scholars resulting in the creation of a template for coding Slavic medieval manuscripts on film. Based on XML (to foster interchange), these MSS records are extremely detailed, and contain not only basic information but also film specifications, and even a 581 field to record titles dealing with the manuscripts described (all this of great value for Slavic scholarship).

Then, in a paper that looks squarely to the future by discussing the development and metadata issues encountered by librarians in the promotion of digital scholarship, Eileen Llona emphasizes the obligation that librarians should feel to retool their existing skills into the kind of expertise that is needed in the digital age: "We don't have to be experts, but we should at least be aware of what it takes to produce digital scholarship . . ." She goes on to observe, "Indeed, this collaboration is often requested by scholars, in terms of having the librarian provide guidance on format and metadata standards, and instruction in the use of such standards, and how to search, access, and cite existing digital projects."

All in all, this volume presents a rich variety of progress reports and new sophistication in the area of *Access to East European and Eurasian Culture: Publishing, Acquisitions, Digitization, Metadata.* The volume is appearing at a time that can be said to mark two significant developments in the field. First, it illustrates the extent of diversification in Eurasian countries as the publishing industry reconstitutes itself and develops exponentially after the upheavals of the late 1980s and early 1990s. Second, it suggests that a watershed may have been reached (1) in the readiness of scholars to adopt new digital technologies in the Slavic field, and (2) in the willingness of Slavic librarians to acquire the expertise to assist them. Judging by the essays in this collection, familiarity with new metadata standards, protocols, and software is already percolating more extensively among Slavic scholars and librarians. It is reflected here not only in methodological essays like Llona's but also in project descriptions: see the references in West, Biggins, et al. (METS, MODS); Zilper and Van Duinen (METS, MODS, OAI-PMH); Hswe (OAI-PMH); and Borodkin and Valetov (PHP/MySQL). But the degree of collaboration between faculty/librarians and librarians/vendors is of even greater note. Whether exemplified by the varied contributions to this volume or more in-depth collaboration on projects, there is a recognition that new advances require a pooling of expertise for proper handling. Long the research model in the sciences, this is now becoming ever more present among Slavic specialists in the humanities, representing a clear maturation of the field.

doi:10.1300/J167v08n02_01

PUBLISHING

The Diversification of Russian Scholarly Publishing, 1995-2005

John Bushnell

SUMMARY. Russian scholarly publication has doubled since 1995, led by private scholarly imprints, which have tripled. The increase in the publication of monographs, in which private publishers now dominate, is particularly noticeable. The majority of private scholarly publication is in history and literary studies, but private presses account for a relatively larger share of publications in philosophy and religion. Scholarly publishing is to a considerable extent funded by a robust network of government and private foundations. doi:10.1300/J167v08n02_02 *[Article copies available for a fee from The Haworth Document Delivery Service: 1-800-HAWORTH. E-mail address: <docdelivery@haworthpress.com> Website:*

John Bushnell, BA, MA, PhD, is Vice President, Russian Press Service (http://www.russianpress.com) and Professor, Department of History, Northwestern University.

Address correspondence to: John Bushnell, 1805 Crain St., Evanston, IL 60202 USA (E-mail: jbushnel@casbah.it.northwestern.edu).

[Haworth co-indexing entry note]: "The Diversification of Russian Scholarly Publishing, 1995-2005." Bushnell, John. Co-published simultaneously in *Slavic & East European Information Resources* (The Haworth Information Press, an imprint of The Haworth Press, Inc.) Vol. 8, No. 2/3, 2007, pp. 7-20; and: *Access to East European and Eurasian Culture: Publishing, Acquisitions, Digitization, Metadata* (ed: Miranda Remnek) The Haworth Information Press, an imprint of The Haworth Press, Inc., 2007, pp. 7-20. Single or multiple copies of this article are available for a fee from The Haworth Document Delivery Service [1-800-HAWORTH, 9:00 a.m. - 5:00 p.m. (EST). E-mail address: docdelivery@haworthpress.com].

Available online at http://seeir.haworthpress.com
© 2007 by The Haworth Press, Inc. All rights reserved.
doi:10.1300/J167v08n02_02

<http://www.HaworthPress.com> © 2007 by The Haworth Press, Inc. All rights reserved.]

KEYWORDS. Publishing, Russia, Russian Academy of Sciences, university presses, monographs, sources, archives, grants

This article is an effort to measure what readers of Russian scholarly books already know: scholarly publishing in the social sciences and humanities has moved well beyond university presses and publishers that are directly connected to the Academy of Sciences and its institutes.

THE DATABASE

Because there are no statistical series that count scholarly books–many of the books that Knizhnaia Palata (Russian Book Chamber) assigns to *philological* and *socioeconomic sciences* are quite unscholarly–I have used a random sample from the Russian Press Service (RPS) database. The sample included books published within Russia and listed in the RPS August and September catalogs for 1995, 1997, 1999, 2001, 2003 and 2005. Two-month samples were taken to even out month-to-month fluctuations in the assortment of publishers represented. Sample years and months were chosen to avoid possible distortions related to the August 1998 Russian default and banking crisis.

But what is a scholarly book? The most obvious type is a monograph presenting original research, but research also appears in collections of scholarly articles, and in the publications of sources–documents and manuscripts–especially if accompanied by at least some of the elements of a scholarly apparatus. Those are the books that I included in the sample: monographs, collections of scholarly articles, and scholarly source publications. The sample excludes translations, republications, textbooks, popularizations, genealogical studies, current memoirs, political tracts, codes of law, and statistics. It also excludes many books of scholarly caliber that might have been included. I did not count any serials except for annuals and a few titles that are published slightly more frequently than once per year; most serials published more frequently would better be considered periodicals, a separate class of scholarly publication. I did not count any *materialy konferentsii* (conference publications) because too often they present research in the form of abstracts or very short articles, and because the research is often unoriginal and unprofessional; this biases the sample against university presses, which frequently publish such volumes. I did not count any volumes in the various *Letopis' zhizni i tvorchestva* (Chronicle of the Life and Work) sets published by the Academy of Sciences, biasing the sample slightly against the Academy. And I did not count encyclopedias, dictionaries, or other reference works–biasing the sample against private publishers that are the major publishers of such volumes–even though many reference texts are undoubtedly of scholarly value. I felt it preferable to exclude such books rather than exaggerate scholarly publishing. The books in the sample represent the core of Russian scholarship.

PUBLISHER CATEGORIES

I assigned publishers to five different categories:

1. Those within or directly related to the Academy of Sciences (the various branches of Nauka, Academy institutes in the humanities and social sciences, Indrik, Nasledie, Peterburgskoe Vostokovedenie, and Dmitrii Bulanin[1]);
2. Universities;
3. Other state institutions (the State History Museum and many other museums, government agencies, Mezhdunarodnaia kniga, and some others);
4. Religious institutions; and
5. Private, commercial presses.

In assigning books to publisher categories, I ignored the Academy (and university) credits sometimes found on the title page of imprints from, for instance, ROSSPEN or Iazyki slavianskoi kul'tury. When I presented a first approximation of this analysis to the 2006 Slavic Librarians workshop at the University of Illinois at Urbana-Champaign, I categorized those books as Academy (or university) publications, following library cataloging practice: any book with the name of the Academy or one of its institutes on the title page is considered an Academy publication. On further reflection, it seemed likely that assignment of these titles to the private press category would provide better insight into the pattern of scholarly publication. It is true that a book with an Academy credit is produced as part of an Academy institute's research and publication plan, has been approved by the institute's academic council, and may have been funded at least in part by the institute in question. On the other hand, the institute may not have paid for publication–the author may have won a publication grant–and an institute scholar is free to publish anywhere he or she chooses, and to declare his/her institute affiliation or not. In any case, the author has agreed to publish with a private press, rather than with an Academy press. Publication credit should reflect authorial choice and publication effort.

The data provided in Table 1 suggest that publication of scholarly titles almost doubled between 1995 and 2005. That rate of increase lags behind the growth of publishing overall, which nearly tripled in the same period, but is a remarkable achievement nonetheless. The bulk of the increase is attributable to commercial presses, which nearly tripled their output of scholarly titles as well as of titles in general. Academy publishing stagnated, although the sudden burst of titles in August-September 2005 may be a harbinger of expansion. University presses produced a gradually rising number of scholarly publications (as well as many textbooks and *materialy konferentsii*) through 2003; the apparent decline in August-September 2005 will probably turn out to be anomalous. The numbers from "other government institutions" and "religious institutions" are too small to support any generalizations, other than that they contributed proportionately less in 2005 than in 1995. But then, all components of scholarly publishing except commercial presses now have a smaller share of the scholarly market than they did in the mid-1990s.

Counting only research monographs (Table 2), it appears that by the mid-1990s commercial firms were publishing roughly the same number as Academy publishers, and more than university presses. By the late 1990s commercial presses were the principal publishers of research monographs, and in the early 2000s published between forty and fifty-three percent of them. Over the entire period 1995-2005, commercial presses tripled their output of research monographs. University and Academy presses produced more in 2005 than in 1995, but with year-to-year variations that suggest that there is no strong trend upwards.

The situation is quite different when it comes to collections of scholarly articles (see Table 3): the Academy leads, universities lag somewhat, while commercial publishers–with the exception of August-September 2005, which may be an anomaly–trail far behind. Academy leadership is easy to explain: most of the Academy serials published in the Soviet period continue (and many Academy journals produce a volume of articles roughly once a year); also Academy institutes produce valuable

TABLE 1. All Scholarly Publications

	Academy	University	Other government organizations	Commercial	Religious institutions	Total
Aug.-Sept. 1995	54	17	15	36	1	123
Aug.-Sept. 1997	52	35	11	36	2	136
Aug.-Sept. 1999	47	41	12	54	0	154
Aug.-Sept. 2001	57	50	15	66	0	188
Aug.-Sept. 2003	48	55	8	53	5	169
Aug.-Sept. 2005	73	36	9	95	2	215

TABLE 2. Research Monographs

	Academy	Universities	Other government organizations	Commercial	Religious institutions	Total
Aug.-Sept. 1995	21	10	2	22	0	57
Aug.-Sept. 1997	20	14	2	17	0	53
Aug.-Sept. 1999	18	22	6	37	0	83
Aug.-Sept. 2001	28	29	10	46	0	113
Aug.-Sept. 2003	25	23	2	41	5	96
Aug.-Sept. 2005	31	19	4	62	0	116

TABLE 3. Collections of Scholarly Articles

	Academy	Universities	Other government institutions	Commercial	Religious institutions	Total
Aug.-Sept. 1995	31	6	2	8	0	47
Aug.-Sept. 1997	29	20	9	14	2	74
Aug.-Sept. 1999	27	19	5	11	0	62
Aug.-Sept. 2001	28	21	5	8	0	62
Aug.-Sept. 2003	21	29	5	6	0	61
Aug.-Sept. 2005	33	16	4	20	2	76

thematic collections of articles by their affiliated scholars. Similarly, universities regularly produce volumes of articles written by their faculty members. The other side of the coin is that commercial presses have not shown much interest in producing volumes of scholarly articles–otherwise much of this type of scholarly output would likely have migrated to commercial presses, just as research monographs have. The reason for that resistance is intuitively clear: collections of miscellaneous articles are not likely to sell as well as a mono- graph with a single subject and a central theme, and are quite unlikely to attract a research or publishing grant from a government or other foundation. Most Russian university press collections of articles are miscellanies, covering many disciplines, topics, and centuries; no commercial press would publish such volumes, whatever the quality of the scholarship. Academy-published collections are more focused, but generally range widely within a single discipline.

It is not really surprising to discover that, as of 1995, commercial presses dominated in the publication of sources, and have since then produced at least half of all such compendia (see Table 4). Pushkin House and other Academy research institutes control mostly manuscripts. Every one of Russia's many state archives controls a larger re-

TABLE 4. Source Publications

	Academy	Universities	Other government institutions	Commercial	Religious institutions	Total
Aug.-Sept. 1995	2	1	2	6	1	12
Aug.-Sept. 1997	3	1	0	5	0	9
Aug.-Sept. 1999	2	0	1	6	0	9
Aug.-Sept. 2001	1	0	0	3	0	4
Aug.-Sept. 2003	2	3	1	6	0	12
Aug.-Sept. 2005	10	1	1	12	0	24

pository of sources than the Academy, but documents from the archives are published by commercial houses rather than by the archives themselves. While there is admittedly some overlap in the types of sources that different groups of publishers produce, in the August-September 2005 RPS catalogs one finds typical Academy publications such as V. D. Zernov, *Zapiski russkogo intelligenta* (Sketches from a Russian Intellectual) (Moscow: Indrik, 2005), a previously unpublished memoir by a scientist who died in 1946; *Dva veka s Pushkinym: materialy ob A. S. Pushkine v fondakh Otdela rukopisei Rossiiskoi natsional'noi biblioteki: katalog* (Two Centuries with Pushkin: Materials about A. S. Pushkin from the Collections of the Manuscript Division of the Russian National Library: Catalog) (St. Petersburg: Dmitrii Bulanin, 2004), which despite the last word in the title consists principally of documents and letters; and *Russkaia sem'ia v vodovorote "Velikogo pereloma:" pis'ma O. A. Tolstoi-Voeikovoi 1927-1929 gg.* (A Russian Family in the Maelstrom of a Great Turning Point: Letters of O. A. Tolstaia-Voeikovaia, 1927 to 1929) (St. Petersburg: Nestor-Istoriia; Russian Academy of Sciences, Institute of History). The same two catalogs offered the following typically private imprints: *Gosudarstvennyi antisemitizm v SSSR: ot nachala do kul' minatsii, 1938-1953* (Government Anti-Semitism in the USSR: From the Beginning to the Culmination, 1938-1953) (Moscow: Materik, 2005); *Sovetskoe voenno-promyshlennoe proizvodstvo, 1918-1926: sbornik dokumentov* (Soviet Military-Industrial Production, 1918-1926: Collection of Documents) (Moscow: Novyi khronograf, 2005); and *RKP(b): vnutripartiinaia bor'ba v dvadtsatye gody: dokumenty i materialy, 1923* (The Russian Communist Party [Bolsheviks]: Internal Party Battle in the Twenties: Documents and Materials, 1923) (Moscow: ROSSPEN, 2004).

Why do the archives not publish their own documents? In fact, why do they not publish their own archival guides?[2] If the case of RGADA (Russian State Archive of Ancient Acts) is representative, the reason stems from a deliberate decision taken by archive directors. The staff at RGADA has urged the director, Mikhail Ryzhenkov, to publish documents from the archive as a way to earn money. But Ryzhenkov has consistently resisted, citing unspecified complications. Instead, RGADA documents have been published in rather small numbers by small private publishers–for instance, by Drevlekhranilishche, basically a one-man operation with an office in the RGADA building but with no institutional or financial ties to RGADA, other than licensing fees to publish the documents. It is quite possible that Ryzhenkov and other archive directors leave publishing issues to private firms because they prefer to avoid involvement with the tax code, or the tax inspectors, who would inevitably descend on the archives if they undertook commercial activity.[3]

As we can see, monographs and sources on the one hand, and collections of articles on the other, are distinctly different sectors of scholarly publication. Monographs (and sources) constitute the more dynamic sector, and are increasingly dominated by private publishers. The Academy and universities publish the overwhelming majority of collections of scholarly articles, and the sector shows no stable growth trend. While it is possible that private publishers will in the future take more of an interest in volumes of articles, there is no particular reason to think that they will. Extrapolating from firmly established trends, it is likely that private publishers will continue to publish increasing numbers of monographs and will become ever more dominant in that segment of the market, while the Academy and universities will continue to publish most volumes of articles, with slow growth in that segment, if any.

WHAT KIND OF WORK ATTRACTS PRIVATE PUBLISHERS?

Scholarly publications can be sorted by discipline as well as by type of publisher and publication. Since it seems to be the case that commercial presses pursue what they want to publish–if they publish little in a particular field, they probably wish to do no more–I treat the statistics below as a measure of the attractiveness of various disciplines to private publishers.

Not surprisingly, commercial publishers have been consistently attracted to works of history and literary studies. In the August and September catalogs for 1999, 2001, 2003, and 2005, works devoted to history (but excluding history of science; see below) accounted for forty-eight, fifty, forty-one, and forty-two percent of private scholarly titles. It seems safe to conclude that history accounts for a steady forty to fifty percent of the scholarly offerings of private presses. Literary studies accounted for eleven, fifteen, thirteen, and twenty-one percent of private scholarly titles. The two fields combined accounted for between fifty-four and sixty-three percent of privately-published scholarly books in the August and September catalogs. In each two-month sample, private publishers outpaced Academy and university publishers in the field of history; in literary studies, private publishers led twice, tied with the Academy once, and fell one title short of the Academy publishers once.

The numbers of publications in all other fields are so small as to be subject to sharp random variation that a two-catalog sample across a six-year period cannot even out, so I measured them across six months (June-November) in 2005. The figures in Table 5 tell us only how private publishers measure up to their Academy and university counterparts, not what percentage of commercially published scholarly books these fields account for.

Despite the strength of private publishing in history and literary studies, private publishers are even stronger in two other fields: philosophy and religion. Of the eighteen scholarly books in philosophy in the catalogs of June-November 2005, twelve (sixty-seven percent) issued from private presses. Of the twenty-six scholarly books in religion listed in the same months, private publishers accounted for sixteen (sixty-two percent). It is true that some of the private presses–such as Palomnik in Moscow–were avowedly Orthodox, but secular publishers like Drevlekhranilishche, Pamiatniki istoricheskoi mysli and Progress-Traditsiia (secular but focused on Russian cultural and religious traditions) accounted for most of the titles.

TABLE 5. Publication of Scholarly Books by Field, 2005
History and Literary Studies: Aug-Sept.; Other Fields: 6 Months

	Academy	University	Other government institutions	Commercial	Religious institutions	Total
Philosophy	4	0	2	12 (67%)	0	18
Religion	4	4	0	16 (62%)	2	26
Literary studies	17	0	0	20 (54%)	0	37
History	31	16	0	40 (46%)	0	87
Economics	9	2	4	8 (34%)	0	23
Archaeology	10	3	1	5 (26%)	0	19
History of Science	14	1	0	5 (25%)	0	20
Ethnography/Folklore	20	11	6	10 (21%)	0	47

Private publishers have comparatively less interest in other fields, though they do publish in all of them. Of twenty-three scholarly publications in economics, private presses contributed eight (thirty-four percent). Of the nineteen scholarly publications in archaeology, private publishers issued five (twenty-six percent). Of the twenty publications in the history of science, they produced only five (twenty-five percent). In the ethnography-folklore category, private publishers produced only ten of forty-seven studies (twenty-one percent). Private publishers' lack of interest in these fields, in some of which there are substantial numbers of scholarly publications, is such that in not one of them do they produce as many scholarly books as they do in the small fields of philosophy and religion.

One reason for commercial publishers' varying interest in different fields is intuitively obvious. Just as they are far more interested in scholarly monographs than in collections of scholarly articles, private publishers are especially interested in history and literary studies because they are marketable: they speak to the current interest in Russia in reassessments of (or arguments about) her national history, and to the interest of many Russians in reevaluations of writers, especially those who were beyond the pale during the Soviet years. By contrast, many scholarly studies in economics have only a narrow professional (or governmental) audience. The relative lack of interest in publishing scholarly works in ethnography and folklore may seem strange, because those related fields should appeal to the public's current interest in Russianness (or Tatarness, Chuvashness, and so forth). The truth is that many of the commercial publications that meet that interest are not scholarly, while genuinely scholarly studies in ethnography and folklore are often too narrow to appeal to the general public. As for archaeology and the history of science, that private publishers have evinced any interest in those fields at all is somewhat surprising. By contrast, private publishers' interest in scholarly studies in religion and philosophy reflects the fact that some of them are committed to the recovery of Russian tradition, and the belief of others that there is a non-academic audience for such publications. A more thorough analysis of the pattern of scholarly publication by commercial presses would produce a useful map of the current interests of what we can still call the Russian intelligentsia.

HOW DO RUSSIAN COMMERCIAL PUBLISHERS SURVIVE? AND WHAT EXACTLY IS A COMMERCIAL PUBLISHER IN THE RUSSIAN CONTEXT?

In the American context, the term *commercial publisher* would be taken as a reference to a publisher who offers at most the occasional scholarly monograph, and whose publishing decisions are by-and-large dictated by a profit motive. Many Russian publishers of scholarly books fit that criterion: Vagrius, a major literary press, for instance; or Academia, which publishes a small number of scholarly studies but is fundamentally a textbook publisher; or Molodaia gvardiia, which publishes many scholarly biographies in its "Zhizn' zamechatel'nykh liudei" (Life of Remarkable People) series, but issues a broad range of non-scholarly books as well. These and many other commercial publishers–Tsentropoligraf, Pskovskaia oblastnaia tipografiia, Respublika, Strelets, Voskresen'e, Os'-89, to name just some from the August 2005 catalog–each produce a few genuinely scholarly books, collectively making a substantial contribution to the total.

However, the mainstays of private scholarly publishing in Russia include what Russians call "elite publishers," which began by aiming at the intelligentsia and subsequently took up publication of works of scholarship, such as Aleteiia in St. Petersburg or Materik in Moscow. They also include publishers like ROSPENN, Iazyki slavianskoi kul'tury, or Progress-Traditsiia, which from the first aimed to publish scholarship. They are commercial in the sense that their income from sales must be greater than their expenses if they are to survive, but they do not aim to maximize profit–they would publish a different sort of book if financial gain were their aim–and have a relatively small target audience.

Every private publisher has a unique story, which most are quite unwilling to tell. Nevertheless, a few patterns can be discerned. Some private presses emerged by stages out of state institutions: Progress-Traditsiia out of the ruins of Progress Publishers, Russkii put' out of a company originally founded by the Library of Foreign Literature and the Pushkin Museum (not the Pushkin Museum of Fine Arts), with a critical contribution from YMCA Press in Paris.[4] Others are mere sidelines of companies whose center of gravity is elsewhere: O.G.I. is part of a firm that operates a chain of restaurants; Ivan Limbakh is an offshoot of a real estate firm; and Limbus Press and U-Faktoriia (Ekaterinburg) are publishing appendages to firms principally involved in printing and other ventures. Others were founded by newly wealthy individuals with a scholarly bent, or found wealthy patrons who could provide the initial capital. Without exception, the stated motivation for founding elite and scholarly presses was non-commercial: to make a contribution to Russian culture and scholarship.[5]

Diversity of provenance aside, all scholarly publishers face the same problem: covering costs while producing books that have a limited market. Most, even those with private wealth at their disposal, draw from the same sources to finance publication: grants from the Russian government and private foundations, contributions from outside Russia, and the authors themselves.

The Russian government provides publication grants from a number of sources, the most important of which is the Russian State Humanities Fund, which has funded a very large number of scholarly publications.[6] The Ministry of Education and Science provides grants through its INO-Tsentr (Informatsiia, Nauka, Obrazovanie [Information, Scholarship, Education]), as does the Federal Agency for the Press and Mass Communication through its "Culture of Russia" program.[7] Other levels of government–some provinces and cities–also provide money for publication, but do not focus specifically on scholarly books. The MacArthur Foundation, the Carnegie Foundation and, until it was shut down, the Russian Soros Foundation have been important foreign sources of funding; many other foreign foundations and institutions have provided at least one-time publishing subventions. Russians, too, have established foundations, many of which provide publishing grants: the Likhachev Fund, the Nabokov Fund, the Pushkin Fund, and the Union of Eurasian Scholars (in effect a foundation to support Eurasian scholars), to name a few. One of the most critical foundations is the International Foundation "Democracy," established by President Yeltsin in 1996 and headed by Aleksandr Iakovlev until his death in October 2005. It has provided very large grants to Materik and other publishing houses to finance the publication of documents on twentieth-century Russian history, but because it is not a government-funded institution it must raise its money from Russian and, especially, foreign contributors.[8]

Absent a grant, some publishers insist that authors themselves pay the cost of publication. It is not clear how widespread this practice is, but according to Nataliia Perova, head of Glas publishers (who provided information on a number of other publishers as well), the director of Tekst, Olgert Libkin, claims that he has never published a book at his own expense.

Without these multiple sources of funding, there would be far less scholarly publishing in Russia, and it would be concentrated in the Academy and university presses. It might seem, therefore, that scholarly publishing is dangerously dependent upon the availability of grants. However, we would need to compare Russian scholarly publishing with publishing in the United States and Europe to determine whether in fact Russian practices differ substantially from those elsewhere. How many American university presses, for instance, receive no subsidies at all from university administrations, and finance themselves entirely through sales? How many American scholars are required to provide university (and other) presses with publication subventions (which they generally obtain from their universities)? It may be that the subsidizing of scholarly publication merely takes a different form in Russia. Furthermore, there is no reason to think that the government programs and private foundations that provide publication grants will disappear; scholarly publication has, after all, grown rapidly in the post-Soviet years, with an increasing rather than a diminishing supply of grants. What seems at first glance to be a patchwork system to support scholarly publication is at present actually quite robust.

NOTES

1. Bulanin is in fact a commercial publisher. However, since Bulanin publishes almost exclusively scholarship issuing from the Academy, and in particular from the Institute of Russian Literature (Pushkin House), because its very *raison d'être* is to provide an outlet for Academy scholarship, and because it would most likely not exist

were it not for the publication of Academy scholarship, its inclusion among the Academy publishers seems reasonable.

2. The handful of exceptions–archives that do publish their own guides–can be found at http://www.rusarchives.ru/publication/list.shtml. The Federal Archives Agency publishes the archival journals *Otechestvennye arkhivy* (Homeland Archives), *Vestnik arkhivista* (Herald of the Archivist), and *Istoricheskii arkhiv* (Historical Archive). One of the few archivally published guides is the four-volume guide to RGADA, published by Glavarkhiv, 1991-1999 and entitled *TSentral'nyi gosudarstvennyi arkhiv drevnikh aktov SSSR: putevoditel v chetyrekh tomakh* (Central State Archive of Ancient Acts of the USSR: Guide in Four Volumes).

3. Vladimir Kozlov, a senior archival official, said this of Rosarkhiv's 1995 decision to abandon early participation in document publication projects with foreign institutions, despite their profitability: "... such 'commerce' did not at all correspond to the status and responsibility of a federal organ of the executive branch ...."; "... almost every day the structural subdivisions of Rosarkhiv [carried out] absolutely inappropriate functions," including accounting; V. P. Kozlov, *Problemy dostupa v arkhivy i ikh ispol'zovaniia: nekotorye razmyshleniia nad opytom raboty rossiiskikh arkhivov 90-kh godov XX veka* (Problems of Archival Use and Access: Some Thoughts on the Work Experience of Russian Archives in the 1990s) (Moscow: Rossiiskoe obshchestvo istorikov-arkhivistov, 2004), 74. Even so, archivists are, of course, deeply involved in location, selection, and preparation of documents for publication.

4. See the Russkii put' web site: http://www.rp-net.ru (accessed July 10, 2006).

5. None of the founders or directors of "elite" and scholarly presses say that their aim was to make a profit or to make a living, although that was in fact what many of them wanted to do. All present themselves as *kulturträger*, which of course they are, and scarcely admit to the fact that they are simultaneously doing business.

6. See Russian State Humanities Fund, http://www.rfh.ru (accessed June 28, 2006).

7. See Podprogramma "Podderzhka poligrafii i knigoizdaniia Rossii (2002-2005 gody)" Federal'noi tselevoi programmy "Kultura Rossii (2002-2005 gody)," http://www.programs-gov.ru/ext/16/1.htm (accessed July 30, 2006).

8. See International Foundation "Democracy," http://www.idf.ru (accessed July 10, 2006).

doi:10.1300/J167v08n02_02

The Slovak Periodical Press: Historical Development, Current Content, New Forms of Access

Peter Olekšák
Albert Kulla

SUMMARY. The authors discuss the development of the Slovak periodical press within its historical context and their expectations for its future. The article covers general characteristics of Slovak magazines and newspapers from World War II to 1989, and their later development since the Velvet Revolution up to the present. It also discusses the Slovak press outside of Slovakia from the late nineteenth century. doi:10.1300/J167v08n02_03 *[Article copies available for a fee from The Haworth Document Delivery Service: 1-800-HAWORTH. E-mail address: <docdelivery@haworthpress.com> Website: <http://www.HaworthPress.com> © 2007 by The Haworth Press, Inc. All rights reserved.]*

KEYWORDS. Slovakia, Slovak, periodical, periodicals, serials, press, newspapers, magazines, before 1989, regional, church, community, censorship, *Pravda, Praca, Narodna obroda,* Slovaks outside Slovakia, Slovak diaspora, compatriot media, Revival Process, Velvet Revolution

---

Peter Olekšák, PhD, is Associate Professor, Department of Journalism, Philosophical Faculty, Catholic University of Ružomberok, Hrabovská cesta 1/1652, 034 01 Ružomberok, Slovakia (E-mail: Peter.Oleksak@fphil.ku.sk).

Albert Kulla, MA, is PhD Candidate, Department of Journalism at the same university and address (E-mail: kulla@fphil.ku.sk).

[Haworth co-indexing entry note]: "The Slovak Periodical Press: Historical Development, Current Content, New Forms of Access." Olekšák, Peter, and Albert Kulla. Co-published simultaneously in *Slavic & East European Information Resources* (The Haworth Information Press, an imprint of The Haworth Press, Inc.) Vol. 8, No. 2/3, 2007, pp. 21-29; and: *Access to East European and Eurasian Culture: Publishing, Acquisitions, Digitization, Metadata* (ed: Miranda Remnek) The Haworth Information Press, an imprint of The Haworth Press, Inc., 2007, pp. 21-29. Single or multiple copies of this article are available for a fee from The Haworth Document Delivery Service [1-800-HAWORTH, 9:00 a.m. - 5:00 p.m. (EST). E-mail address: docdelivery@haworthpress.com].

Available online at http://seeir.haworthpress.com
© 2007 by The Haworth Press, Inc. All rights reserved.
doi:10.1300/J167v08n02_03

INTRODUCTION

A small country (5.5 million inhabitants) in Central Europe, Slovakia borders on the Czech Republic and Austria in the west, Poland in the north, Ukraine in the east, and Hungary in the south. It is a young country with an eventful past. It was part of the Austro-Hungarian Empire until 1918, then part of the Czechoslovak Republic until 1938. In that year, Slovakia became a separate state controlled by Nazi Germany. After World War II, it once again united with the Czech lands to become part of Czechoslovakia. Slovakia and the Czech Republic went their separate ways after January 1, 1993, and in May 2004 Slovakia became a member of the European Union.

The periodical press, including newspapers and magazines, has always been a part of the country's history. It has monitored the various forms of state establishments and political systems: empire, democracy, fascism, socialism, and efforts toward communism, as well as attempts to make democratic reforms.

THE PERIODICAL PRESS BEFORE 1989

Immediately after World War II, Czechoslovakia was reassembled and came under the influence of the Soviet Union and its Warsaw Pact. From the year 1948 onward, there existed neither freedom of the press nor private property–not only for the media but also for publishing companies and printers. The periodical press belonged exclusively to the state and the party; only selected parties of the so-called Národný front (National Group of Armies) could publish their own newspapers.

Thus the Democratic Party published the daily *Čas* (Time), from 1944 to 1948; the weekly *Čas v obrazoch* (Time in Pictures), 1946-1948; the regional newspaper *Demokrat* (The Democrat), 1945-1948; and *Demokratické hlasy* (Democratic Voices), 1945-1946. The party Slovenská obroda published the daily *L'ud* (The People), which also continued after 1948, with a circulation of 20,000 copies. The Party of Liberty published the daily *Sloboda* (Liberty), 1946-1948, which became a weekly; the regional newspapers *Československý východ* (The Czechoslovak East), *Ciel'* (Aim), and *Dedina* (The Village) were published for a short period. Another twenty regional, church, or community periodicals were published between 1945 and 1948; they ceased or suffered strict censorship after the Communist coup in 1948.

The Slovak Communist Party published a wide range of newpapers and magazines: the daily *Pravda* (Truth); *Východoslovenská pravda* (*Eastern-Slovak Pravda*) in the east, 1945-1952; *Hlas ľudu* (Voice of the People), 1945-1950; the weekly *Roľnícka nedeľa* (Agricultural Sunday), 1946; and *Nové slovo* (The New Word), 1952.

The Slovak National Council (the national parliament) began to publish *Národná obroda* (National Revival) in 1945, but it was soon closed. Meanwhile the army produced the daily *Bojovník* (The Warrior), *Obrana vlasti* (Defence of the Motherland), and *Svobodné Československo* (Free Czechoslovakia), but they too were shortlived. True, the unions published the daily *Práca* (Work) from 1946, and it was published throughout the Communist period.[1] But in general these unfavorable press conditions remained nearly the same until 1989, with the exception of the short, so-called Revival Process in the 1960s, which was forcefully ended by the Warsaw Pact army during the night of August 20-21, 1968.

A gradual loosening took place in the mid-1980s, after Mikhail Gorbachev became leader of the Communist Party in the Soviet Union. The first demonstration against the regime, the so-called Candle Manifestation, took place on Good Friday, March 25, 1988. It was dispersed by the police. There was a confrontation of the two fronts on November 16, 1989, during a demonstration of university students in Bratislava, and again on November 17, in Prague. This open conflict between young people and the political powers was the beginning of the Velvet Revolution, which heralded freedom of the press in our country.

THE PERIODICAL PRESS AFTER THE VELVET REVOLUTION IN CZECHOSLOVAKIA (1989)

The political changes of November 1989 were mirrored in the composition of the Slovak press as well. Freedom of the press and free enterprise stimulated the birth of a large number of new titles, a development that is described in the work of Danuša Serafínová.[2] Categories of the press that had, for the most part, been suppressed by the regime prior to November 1989 were now permitted, e.g., church titles. New publishing companies arose that faced the full risk of the market. Many of the new periodicals survived for only a short period, but additional new titles filled the vacuum after them.[3] Foreign capital gradually entered the Slovak media market.[4] Slovak periodical publishers include: Perit Press PLC, Ringier Slovakia, Spoločnosť 7 Plus, Perex, Ecopress, and Vydavateľstvo Živena.

The Daily Press

At the time of the Velvet Revolution, twelve daily newspapers were being published in Slovakia. Some new dailies were added to them, e.g., *Národná Obroda* (National Revival), *Nový Slovák* (The New Slovak), *Slovenský denník* (Slovak Daily), *Verejnosť* (The Public), *Koridor* (The Corridor), etc. *Verejnosť*, the organ of the revolutionary movement Verejnosť proti násiliu (The Public Against Violence), ceased publication after the creation of the Slovak Republic. Many others followed suit, with the exception of *Národná Obroda*. *Slovenský denník*, the organ of the Christian Democratic movement, survived until 1994.

Nový Čas (New Time) is a tabloid and the best-selling daily in Slovakia. Its content is gutter press. As of 2005, its print run was 190,000. The widely read supplement *Nový Čas víkend* (*Nový Čas* Weekend) is added on Sundays.

Pravda is a major newspaper in Slovakia. In the past, it was the Slovak equivalent of the Soviet *Pravda*. Since the Velvet Revolution, however, it has acquired a modern neutral voice and is one of the most important Slovak newspapers.

Sme (We Are) is a very influential Slovak daily.[5] Its target group is very broad, but officially it focuses on the general public and on intellectuals.

Both the daily *Sport* and the Hungarian minority daily *Új Szó* (New Word) were published before 1989, but they have changed their images completely. They are popular with readers.

Hospodarske noviny (Economic Newspaper) is a daily that concentrates on economic news.

The daily *Práca*, which was published during the Communist period, continued after the Velvet Revolution until 2002 when, as noted earlier, it merged with the daily *Sme*.[6] It was an elite newspaper, but at the same time it was among the most popular with readers. Its subject matter included union issues.

Korzar, the daily of the city of Košice, is the most successful among the regional and local dailies. It has been published since 1998 as a successor to *Korzo*.

It has become established practice within the last few years for both large dailies and those of lesser circulation to have online versions. Additional recent developments are discussed elsewhere, e.g., Imrich Jenča has written about changes in journalism, and Peter Olekšák has investigated the print media.[7]

The Weekly Press

As of 2000, 134 weekly papers were being published in Slovakia, of which forty-four were national, seventy-nine regional, and eleven local. This number indicates a much greater variety than in the period before November 1989, and a discussion of all of them would require several pages.

Among the most successful national pictorial weeklies today are social and family magazines and publications devoted to TV programs. In addition to traditional family magazines like *Život* (Life) and *Slovenka* (Slovak Woman), which are published for women, readers also enjoy social journals, e.g., *Plus 7 dní* (Plus Seven Days) and *Markíza*, a TV program magazine that carries articles about famous show business personalities; it appeals chiefly to young people. *Eurotelevízia* (Eurotelevision) and the Hungarian *Vasárnap* (Sunday) are among the ten most popular weeklies. *Katolícke noviny* (Catholic Newspaper), a journal of the Catholic Church, places in the top ten as well. We should also mention such local magazines as *Liptov* in Liptovský Mikuláš, *Kysuce* in Čadca, and the bilingual Slovak and Hungarian magazine *Komárňanské listy = Komáromi Lápok* in Komárno, as well as the specialized *Šport Expres* in Michalovce. Weekly periodicity is also typical of the free advertisement newspapers that often appear in our mailboxes, e.g., *Titan*.

The Monthly Press

As far as monthly periodicals are concerned, the most popular in Slovakia cover the family, women, advice, and entertainment. Examples are *Rebecca, Eva, Ženský magazín* (Women's Magazine), *Minikrížovky* (Mini-Crosswords), *Záhradkár* (The Gardener), and *Zdravie* (Health). Many readers subscribe to *Reader's Digest Výber* (Reader's Digest Selections), which brings entertainment and advice. Sports fans read *Šport revue*, and history enthusiasts read *Historická revue* (Historical Review). *Karpathenblatt*, the journal of the German minority, is also a monthly.

As of 2000, there were 170 bimonthlies, 219 quarterlies, and seventy with other periodicities, in addition to the daily, weekly, and monthly periodicals. The year 2004 was rich in the creation of new periodicals, e.g., the social monthlies *Live!* and *Týždeň* (The Week), together with additional successful magazines for women, like *Šarm* (Charm), *Báječná žena* (Wonderful Woman), *Nový čas pre ženy* (New Time for Women), or the previously mentioned *Rebecca*.

The Slovak Diaspora Press [8]

There are more than two million Slovaks living abroad: in Europe, North and South America, Africa, and Australia. They emigrated during recent centuries because of poverty and a search for escape from political regimes. They became devoted citizens of their adopted countries, but they remained–and still remain–in contact with their homeland by means of periodicals in the language of their ancestors. The number, periodicity, and format of these publications depend on the extent of the Slovak community at a given time and place. Historical and current émigré serials show a picture of the whole Slovak community, which is often scattered.

At the end of the nineteenth and beginning of the twentieth centuries, Slovaks, mostly from the eastern part of their territory, emigrated in large numbers to work in America. The first periodical with the goal of helping Slovaks in the United States was *Bulletin*, established by J. Slovenský and J. Wolf in 1885. The next year, Slovenský founded *Amerikánszko-slovenské noviny* (American-Slovak Newspaper) in Pittsburgh, Pennsylvania. These publications were written in the Sharish dialect. *Nová vlast'* (New Motherland) was the first émigré newspaper written in literary Slovak; it was established in 1888. One year later, a weekly called *Slovák v Amerike* (Slovak in America) began publication in Middletown, Pennsylvania. It is now the oldest Slovak periodical in America.

During the Hapsburg period, Slovak periodicals in the United States were published by both lay people and clergy. For instance, the title *Katolícke noviny* (Catholic Newspaper) was established by Rev. Ignác Jaškovič, founder of the first Slovak parish in the U.S., the parish of Saint John in Hazleton, Pennsylvania. In 1911, *Katolícky sokol* (Catholic Falcon) began publication; it is now called *Slovak Catholic Falcon*.

The American Bulletin began in 1918 as the organ of American Czechoslovak National Council in Chicago. Newspapers were published also in many other cities with Slovak communities. Before the end of World War I, American Slovaks had more dailies than their compatriots in Slovakia.

The first Canadian Slovak newspaper was published in Blaimore under the title *Slovenské slovo* (Slovak Word) in 1910 and 1911. *Kanadské noviny* (Canadian Newspaper) began publication in 1929.

Additional periodicals published in the United States are: *Americký slovák* (American Slovak); the Catholic fraternal weekly *Jednota* (Union), based in Cleveland; and the monthly *Ženská jednota* (Ladies' Union), the organ of the First Catholic Ladies Union, which began in 1914.

Most Slovak émigré periodicals began after World War II, when Slovakia was incorporated into the socialist bloc and many dissenting Slovaks saved themselves from persecution by escaping into exile. Slovaks living in Hungary, Poland, and Yugoslavia likewise found themselves in the socialist bloc.

The Slovak diaspora press took two forms. One was democratic. Examples include *Slovenský štít* (Slovak Shield), begun in Australia in 1950; *La Vie* (Life), started in France in 1956 by the Slovak Catholic Mission; *Slovenské hlasy z Ríma* (Slovak Voices), begun in Rome in 1952; *Kanadský slovák* (The Canadian Slovak), begun in 1942. These periodicals, along with U.S. titles, especially *Slovák v Amerike* (The Slovak in America), were considered reactionary by journalists in Slovakia.

The second form, published by Slovaks living elsewhere in the eastern bloc, was subject to control by the Communist Party. The party considered these periodicals to be obedient servants of the regime. *L'udové noviny* (Popular Newspaper) was published in this way beginning in 1957. Slovaks in Poland began *Krajanský život* (Compatriot Life) in 1956 and *Život* (Life) in 1958.

Among more recent U.S. publications are the *Slovak American Newsletter*, published three times per year since 1991 for members of the Slovak American Cultural Society of the Midwest, and the quarterly *Floridský slovák* (Floridian Slovak).

The large number of Slovak-language periodicals still being published outside Slovakia show that despite the wide opportunities presented by the Internet and despite their ability to speak foreign languages, Slovaks living abroad still like to read print publications in their mother tongue.

THE FUTURE

We expect publishing companies in Slovakia to become stronger in the near future, but at the same time we also anticipate shifts in the proprietors' relations with the print media. We also believe that electronic versions of dailies, weeklies, and monthlies will become more numerous.[9] This trend will take place only as rapidly as families gain Internet connections. But we expect that in the future, about eighty percent of households will have the possibility to read daily newspapers online.

As far as libraries and resource centers are concerned, access to virtual libraries across the world and digitization of Slovak books and serials are only in their infancy. Since 2000, university libraries have been making PDF versions of their students' theses for degrees of all levels, as well as PDF versions of their own publications.

According to a press release of June 7, 2006, the Slovak National Library plans to build a digital center and scan 350,000 volumes from its stacks. The 122 million pages will be scanned with special scanners, which will be bought with European grants if necessary. The digitizing is scheduled to begin in December 2008.

NOTES

1. *Práca* continued to be published well after 1989. However, in 1999 the German publisher Verlagsgruppe Passau became the co-owners of the daily *Sme*, and then acquired *Práca*. They published the same contents in both dailies in the same format, and in consequence merged the two: as of June 2, 2002, the daily *Sme* has been published with the secondary title *Práca*. A similar situation occurred with *Národná obroda*, which began again after the Velvet Revolution; it was later bought up, and then ceased on June 1, 2005.

2. Danuša Serafínová and Jozef Vatrál, *Náčrt dejín slovenskej žurnalistiky* (Outline of the History of Slovak Journalism), 158-163 (Ružomberok: Katolícka univerzita v Ružomberku, 2000).

3. Imrich Jenča, "Novinári a zdroje informácií" (Journalists and Sources of Information), in *Vývoj žurnalistiky na Slovensku po 17. novembri 1989* (The Influence of Journalism in Slovakia After November 17, 1989), 57-68 (Ružomberok: Katolícka univerzita v Ružomberku, 2004).

4. Michal Dyttert, "Stav televízneho spravodajstva po 15 rokoch od začiatku slobodnej žurnalistiky na Slovensku" (The State of Television Newscasting Fifteen Years after the Beginning of Free Journalism in Slovakia), in *Vývoj žurnalistiky na Slovensku po 17. novembri 1989*, 41-50 (Ružomberok: Katolícka univerzita v Ružomberku, 2004).

5. *Sme* has been published since January 6, 1993. Its entire editorial staff was formerly responsible for the daily *Smena*, but due to state involvement in its editorial matters after the formation of the Slovak Republic on January 2, 1993, the staff left and immediately started the new daily *Sme* later that same week.

6. Peter Olekšák, *Vzt'ah cirkvi a štátu na Slovensku v rokoch 1999-2000 ako ho prezentovali denníky Sme a Slovenská republika* (The Relationship Between Church and State in Slovakia in the Years 1999-2000, As Presented in the Dailies *Sme* and *Slovenská republika*) (Ružomberok: Katolícka univerzita v Ružomberku, 2000).

7. Imrich Jenča, "Zmeny novinárskej profesie" (Changes in the Journalistic Profession), *Otázky žurnalistiky* 46, no. 1-2 (2003), 97-98; Peter Olekšák, *Medzištátna zmluva medzi Svätou stolicou a Slovenskou republikou v ohlasoch masmédií* (Bilateral Agreement Between the Holy See and the Slovak Republic as Reflected in the Mass Media) (Ružomberok: Katolícka univerzita v Ružomberku, 2005).

8. See Pavol Holeštiak, *Slovenské médiá vo svete* (Slovak Media in the World) (Čadca: Vzlet, 2002).

9. Juraj Považan, *Príspevok k výskumu využitia nových technológii v žurnalistickej praxi*. (Contribution to an Investigation of the Use of New Technologies in Journalistic Work) (Ružomberok: Katolícka univerzita v Ružomberku, 2006).

doi:10.1300/J167v08n02_03

ACQUISITIONS

Iltimos, bizga kitoblar yuboring! U.S. Libraries' Collecting Strategies for Central Asian Publications

Karen Rondestvedt

SUMMARY. There are between fifteen and twenty U.S. libraries that collect publications from Central Asia, defined here as Kazakhstan, Kyrgyzstan, Tajikistan, Turkmenistan and Uzbekistan. Collection development responsibility for these countries tends to rest with the Slavic selector, the Middle East selector, or both, divided by language. Vendors who can supply this material mostly also supply publications from other countries of the former Soviet Union. The author briefly discusses the history of collecting from this region and the results of a survey con-

---

Karen Rondestvedt, MA, MLS, PhD, is Curator for Slavic and East European Collections, Stanford University Libraries, 345A Green Library, Stanford, CA 94305-6004 USA (E-mail: rondest@stanford.edu).

[Haworth co-indexing entry note]: *"Iltimos, bizga kitoblar yuboring!* U.S. Libraries' Collecting Strategies for Central Asian Publications." Rondestvedt, Karen. Co-published simultaneously in *Slavic & East European Information Resources* (The Haworth Information Press, an imprint of The Haworth Press, Inc.) Vol. 8, No. 2/3, 2007, pp. 31-47; and: *Access to East European and Eurasian Culture: Publishing, Acquisitions, Digitization, Metadata* (ed: Miranda Remnek) The Haworth Information Press, an imprint of The Haworth Press, Inc., 2007, pp. 31-47. Single or multiple copies of this article are available for a fee from The Haworth Document Delivery Service [1-800-HAWORTH, 9:00 a.m. - 5:00 p.m. (EST). E-mail address: docdelivery@haworthpress.com].

Available online at http://seeir.haworthpress.com
© 2007 by The Haworth Press, Inc. All rights reserved.
doi:10.1300/J167v08n02_04

ducted in 2004. She presents evidence indicating that the main reason U.S. libraries are not receiving more books from the region is most likely because they are not being published, not because vendors are doing an inadequate job. doi:10.1300/J167v08n02_04 *[Article copies available for a fee from The Haworth Document Delivery Service: 1-800-HAWORTH. E-mail address: <docdelivery@haworthpress.com> Website: <http://www.HaworthPress. com> © 2007 by The Haworth Press, Inc. All rights reserved.]*

KEYWORDS. Central Asia, Kazakhstan, Kyrgyzstan, Tajikistan, Turkmenistan, Uzbekistan, United States, books, libraries, acquisition, collecting, publishing

As the title says beggingly in Uzbek, "Please send us books!" There are between fifteen and twenty U.S. libraries that collect publications from Central Asia, defined for present purposes as Kazakhstan, Kyrgyzstan, Tajikistan, Turkmenistan, and Uzbekistan. This article discusses the history of collecting strategies from these countries and changes in collecting strategies since independence in 1992. It then addresses the perception that we are not receiving as many publications from the region as we should be, expressed both informally and in the survey to be discussed in the section "Survey of U.S. Libraries" and Appendix 2, by looking at publishing in the five countries. The focus is on monographs.

COLLECTING STRATEGIES DURING SOVIET TIMES

In Soviet days, most U.S. libraries had two main strategies for obtaining Central Asian publications: buying them from a Western vendor that dealt with Mezhdunarodnaia kniga, the Soviet book export monopoly; or receiving them via exchange from one of the few Soviet libraries permitted to supply books and receive them from the West. The names of Western vendors of the time will be familiar to anyone who was in the field twenty years ago: Les Livres Etrangers, Kamkin, Kubon & Sagner, Collets, and a few others. In my own experience, the best exchange partner supplier of Central Asian publications was the State Public Historical Library in Moscow, which was in general the best exchange supplier of Soviet books published outside of Moscow and Leningrad. But other large Moscow and Leningrad libraries could also supply Central Asian titles: for example, the Library for Foreign Literature, the Lenin Library (now the Russian State Library), and the Saltykov-

Shchedrin Library (now the Russian National Library). It is also likely that the library of the Siberian Branch of the USSR Academy of Sciences in Novosibirsk was able to supply some Central Asian material to exchange partners.

Material of interest to research libraries and available through these strategies was often published by government-funded and government-controlled learned societies and academic institutions, and the publications themselves were subsidized by the government. Material supplied by one of the vendors had passed some sort of censorship, had entered the book trade, and had been deemed acceptable for export. Exchange partners could supply some material that had not entered the book trade and some that had not been deemed acceptable for export.

The very largest libraries also employed a third means of acquisition: collection on the spot–by the American librarian, by his or her agent(s), or by an overseas office. The success of this method depended on the political climate in the Soviet Union at the time, export regulations, and the skill and derring-do of the people involved.

COLLECTING DURING GLASNOST' AND PERESTROIKA

Beginning with the *glasnost'* and *perestroika* period in the second half of the 1980s and accelerating with the breakup of the Soviet Union at the end of 1991, U.S. libraries were forced to change acquisition tactics or they would receive little or nothing. One by one, beginning with Les Livres Etrangers, the vendors whose business depended primarily on Mezhdunarodnaia kniga went out of business. New vendors arose to fill the vacuum, including ATC Books International, East View Publications (now East View Information Services), Russia Online, and Russian Press Service in the U.S.; Buchversand Krieger in Germany; and Moscow Independent Press Publications (now MIPP International), based in Minsk.

While exchange partner libraries located in Russia could, at least theoretically, provide Central Asian books during the 1986-1991 period, they themselves stopped receiving Central Asian books via either obligatory deposit or the bibkollektor[1] when the Soviet Union disintegrated.

COLLECTING SINCE INDEPENDENCE

Since the Soviet Central Asian republics became five independent nations in 1992, U.S. libraries have been working to find the most effective collecting strategy or strategies for material from those countries. Many of the new vendors that arose during *glasnost'* and *perestroika* to supply books from the Soviet Union are still very much alive and supplying books from all or most of the former Soviet republics. Particularly strong with Central Asian publications as of this writing are, in alphabetical order: ATC Books International, Buchversand Krieger, East View Information Services, MIPP International, and Russia Online. In fact, those vendors collectively have become the single most important source for Central Asian books for U.S. research libraries. (Up-to-date contact information for all vendors mentioned can be found in the database *Sources for Slavic and East European Library Materials*, http://library.arizona.edu/slavvend/.) To the best of my knowledge, all of these vendors have agents in Central Asia who supply them with books.

Middle Eurasian Books in Lac-Beauport, Quebec is a special case. According to the owner, Oleg Semikhnenko, the firm was founded in 1996 to procure hard-to-get books from the former Soviet Union. They obtain most of their material through occasional personal visits.[2] Their stock, listed on their website (http://www.meabooks.com/), may include material that other vendors cannot supply.

Survey of U.S. Libraries

During several months in 2004, I conducted a survey of U.S. libraries' collecting of Central Asian publications. I used the e-mail list *Slavlibs* as a starting point and asked list members to pass the survey on to the proper colleague at their institution if they themselves were not responsible for collecting from those countries. The motivation for survey was a visit to Stanford by Will Tuchrello, who at that time was the Library of Congress (LC)'s Field Director for Southwest Asia, based in Islamabad, Pakistan. Tuchrello was exploring the possibility of setting up an LC collecting operation for material from one or more of the former Soviet Central Asian countries. He wanted to gauge how many other libraries might be interested in receiving material from such an office and which countries were the most problematic. Eighteen libraries responded to the survey and updated results have been incorporated into the following section (Summary of Current Collecting), and into Appendix 2.

As of this writing (August 2006), no LC operation for collecting Central Asian publications has been established, probably for reasons internal to LC. However, our vendors also continue to provide reasonable service.

Summary of Current Collecting

Collection development for the Central Asian countries is handled in three ways among U.S. libraries:

- Slavic librarian(s) responsible for all of it
- Middle East librarian(s) responsible for all of it
- Responsibility divided by language, with Slavic librarian handling Slavic and, in many cases, Western languages; and the Middle East librarian handling vernaculars

U.S. libraries that collect Central Asian material can be divided into four groups according to their collecting patterns.

- Group 1. The following libraries, in alphabetical order, report collecting a full range of subjects (including belles lettres), in local languages as well as in Russian and Western languages, from all five countries: Columbia University, Indiana University, Library of Congress, New York Public Library, University of California–Berkeley, University of Chicago, University of Illinois–Urbana–Champaign, University of Michigan, University of Washington, and University of Wisconsin-Madison. Harvard University almost certainly falls into this category as well. Librarians at Widener report collecting from all five countries in all applicable languages, in a full range of subjects except for music, art, and anthropology. That exception is because other libraries on campus collect those subjects. The websites of Tozzer Library (anthropology), the Loeb Music Library, and the Fine Arts Library suggest, but don't state explicitly, that they may collect some material from Central Asia.
- Among the highlights from this first group, the University of Illinois has a large collection of newspapers from Central Asia, 111 titles. Several librarians said that belles lettres and folkore were especially important to collect in the vernaculars. Managers of some large collections mentioned collecting material not only in the languages of the countries, but also in such minority languages as Altay, Bashkir, Chuvash, Tatar, Uighur, Sakha, and Tuvan.[3]

- Group 2. The libraries in this group collect broadly but not in all social science and humanities subjects; in local languages, Russian, and Western languages; and from all five countries. The University of Kansas collects from all five countries in all applicable languages, in a full range of subjects with the apparent exception of belles lettres. Stanford University, which took over much of this collecting from the Hoover Institution, acquires from all five countries in all applicable languages, in a full range of subjects with the exception of belles lettres and literary criticism.
- Group 3. Libraries in this group collect from all five countries, in a broad range of subjects, but only in Russian and Western languages: Duke University and University of North Carolina–Chapel Hill.
- Group 4. This group consists of libraries that collect selectively in one way or another. The Hoover Institution, since 2001, has acquired only archival material, pamphlets, and ephemera in its subject areas, which emphasize twentieth-century history and politics. Theoretically, it acquires material from Central Asia, but the curator responsible has been out on disability for over a year. The University of Iowa acquires mostly from Kazakhstan, selectively, in Russian. The University of Texas at Austin reports collecting selectively in the vernacular from Tajikistan, and selectively from the others in English and, occasionally, in Russian.

When asked which countries were the most problematic from the standpoint of acquiring material, most librarians answering the survey mentioned Turkmenistan, Tajikistan, or–often–both. A few said they were all equally problematic.

DO U.S. LIBRARIES REALLY HAVE A PROBLEM ACQUIRING CENTRAL ASIAN PUBLICATIONS?

Is there material being published that we should be acquiring, but we're not? Does lack of material from a country mean that our vendors are doing an inadequate job? It is difficult to answer either question definitively, but this section will discuss what I believe is the main reason for the low number of Central Asian books reaching us.

It appears that the most important explanation for lack of material from these countries coming to our libraries is that it is not being published. Up-to-date publishing statistics from Central Asia are not always available. The countries are not members of the International

Publishers Association, and recent material published by their statistical services often does not include book production. The *United Nations Statistics Division Common Database* (http://unstats.un.org/unsd/cdb/cdb_help/cdb_quick_start.asp) has figures for all the countries except Turkmenistan, but only from the late 1990s. Thus the documentation presented here is not ideal, but I believe that the picture that emerges is clear.

Let us look at the publishing situation in general in each country, starting with the most problematic and continuing in descending order of acquisition difficulty. Publishing statistics, where available, will be compared to holdings shown in the online catalogs of three U.S. libraries (Harvard, Stanford, and the Library of Congress).

Turkmenistan

Turkmenistan is the smallest of the Central Asian countries, with a population of five million. The political and book situation is so dire that it sounds like a parody of itself. President Saparmurat Niyazov has emptied libraries and bookstores, burned books, and closed most libraries. He is reported in the *IFLA Journal* as having stated that "nobody reads books or goes to libraries." The educational system concentrates its curriculum on the study of the president's Rukhnama ideology, and state bookstores sell only books that support that ideology. In 2005, the Turkmen Helsinki Foundation and Human Rights Watch assessed Turkmenistan as "among the world's most repressive and dictatorial regimes."[4]

A search in English for book publishing in Turkmenistan conducted in East View's *CIS & Baltic Periodicals* database on May 18, 2006 produced 52 hits, most of them not relevant to the topic discussed here. Of the first 20, which comprise the first page of hits in relevance-ranked order, 10 relate to publications by or about Niyazov and three announce books of Turkmen folk legends or proverbs. The most striking hit has this headline: "Turkmen President Sends his Book *Rukhnama* to Space." A search in Russian produced considerably less. The most relevant article concerns Turkmenistan's participation at the Leipzig Book Fair, where the "powerful process of national renaissance" since independence was showcased.[5] No publishing statistics since independence in 1992 were found.

This material strongly suggests that almost nothing of interest to a research library is being published in Turkmenistan.

Tajikistan

With a population of a little over seven million, Tajikistan is one of the three small Central Asian countries (with Turkmenistan and Kyrgyzstan), and like Turkmenistan is considered one of the most problematic of these countries in terms of acquisitions. Its civil war, which lasted from 1992 to 1997, severely damaged its already fragile economy. Since 1997, the economy has been growing steadily, but 64% of the population still lives in abject poverty, according to the *CIA World Factbook*. In addition, there is ample evidence of a repressive government that tightly controls publishing.[6]

Are there Tajik government and government-approved publications that U.S. research libraries would want but are not receiving? At the end of May 2006, Stanford's online catalog showed 127 titles published in Dushanbe during the period 2000-2006. Of those, one was published in 2006, 16 in 2005, 21 in 2004, 29 in 2003, 23 in 2002 (of which three were still on order), 25 in 2001, and 12 in 2000. Receipts, in other words, have been sparse, slow in coming, and fairly consistent, at least starting in 2001. At the same time, Harvard's HOLLIS catalog showed 140 titles published in Dushanbe during the same period, and the Library of Congress's showed 228.

Recent publishing statistics are available for Tajikistan. Figures from the Tajik statistical yearbook of 2005 are extracted in Table 1. These numbers are not in tens or hundreds, but in single units.[7]

Given that there were only 1,196 monographic titles published in the period 2000-2004, the 110 that Stanford acquired from that period (9.2% of the publishing output) are probably about what we should have acquired. LC acquired 19.0% of the reported output, and Harvard 11.7%.

Using another method, I compared Stanford's holdings of Tajik statistical publications to what is listed on the website of the State Statistical Committee of Tajikistan (http://www.stat.tj/english/home.htm in English and http://www.stat.tj/index.htm in Russian), and found that

TABLE 1. Book Publishing in Tajikistan

Item	1991	1999	2000	2001	2002	2003	2004
Books & brochures (printed units)	723	189	180	212	270	250	284

we are receiving most of the statistical serials we would want–from East View and ATC. Surprisingly, I did not find any Tajik statistical serials in East View's serials database at the end of May 2006–even titles they are sending to us. But a search for *Tadzhikistan* and *Tojikiston* produced a number of non-statistical government serials Stanford is not receiving, including legal acts of parliament (*Akhbori Majlisi Olii Jumkhurii Tojikiston*) and Legal Acts of the President and the Cabinet of Ministers (*Farmon va amrkhoi Prezident, karor va amrkhoi Khukumati Jumkhurii Tojikiston = Sobranie reshenii prezidiuma i kabineta ministrov Tadzhikskoi Respubliki*). Each is monthly and each is over $500.00. The database shows that a number of serials from the Academy of Sciences have been suspended.

Uzbekistan

Lists of available books from the vendors mentioned earlier suggest that U.S. libraries are receiving an abundance of Uzbek publications, especially when the number of Uzbek books on offer is compared to the number of Turkmen and Tajik titles offered. However, Uzbekistan has a population of over twenty-seven million, five million more than Romania; yet the number of Uzbek publications on offer does not begin to approach the number of Romanian publications that we see from vendors like DEREX. Thus U.S. libraries are actually seeing a lack of publications from Uzbekistan as well.

Does the lack of Uzbek publications on offer mean that our vendors are performing inadequately? Such a conclusion would be wrong, since statistics show that the rate of publishing per capita in Uzbekistan is also quite low. In the most recent publishing statistics I could find for the country, for 1996, the total number of books was given as 1,003. In contrast, the total listed for Romania in 1996 was 7,199.[8]

The low rate of publishing in Uzbekistan seems to be the result of a combination of a number of factors: repressive government, labyrinthine regulations, corruption, and the poverty of most of the population. An Uzbek colleague familiar with the current situation provided some impressionistic information about Uzbek publishing in May 2006. There are a handful of state-run publishers that publish everything "legal." There are also some private publishers, but they have a difficult time surviving. Government bookstores sell only books published by the state-run publishers. *Bukinist*s, or book stands on the street, sell all kinds of books, including used ones. New books are quite expensive for most people: the equivalent of three to six dollars, when the average salary is 25 to 40 dollars per month. Books about current affairs are usually published by NGOs such as Soros, IREX, and UNDP (United Nations Development Programme). Such material comes out in small print runs and only people involved with those NGOs can obtain them. Private businesses of all kinds need to pay production tax, income tax, and bribes in order to continue operation.[9]

Kazakhstan

Kazakhstan is by far the largest Central Asian country by area, but its population is only fifteen million, 56% of Uzbekistan's. Still, despite this relatively small number (although it is the second largest Central Asian country by population), Kazakhstan published–according to the U.N. database–1,223 book titles in 1999. That number is 22% more than Uzbekistan published in 1996. The number of Kazakh publications has almost certainly increased since then, although more recent figures are not readily available.

The *CIA World Factbook* describes the Kazakh government as "authoritarian presidential rule." But it also reports that the Kazakh economy has been improving rapidly: nine percent growth or more per year from 2002 to 2005, due in large part to its "booming energy sector, but also to economic reform, good harvests, and foreign investment." The government has also been encouraging publishing and the book trade. For example, several book fairs have taken place in the country beginning in 2001, including three international fairs called "Along the Great Silk Way" ("Po velikomu shelkovomu puti"). The first one was attended by individuals and firms from Azerbaijan, China, Germany, Great Britain, Hungary, Kazakhstan, Kyrgyzstan, Mongolia, The Netherlands, Russia, Tajikistan, Turkey, and Ukraine.[10]

Stanford and Hoover together acquired 66 publications from Kazakhstan published in 1999. (This was before Central Asia became such a high priority for Stanford.) For the same year, LC's online catalog shows 280 from Almaty/Alma Ata, Astana, and Karaganda/Qaraghandy (ca. 23% of the publication output); and Harvard's catalog shows 119 from the same cities (9.7%). For 2003 publications from Almaty and Astana, the main publishing centers, Stanford has 110, LC has 288, and Harvard has 46. For 2004 publications from the same cities, Stanford has 100, LC has 220, and Harvard has 84. These holdings figures suggest that the amount of material the three libraries received from Kazakhstan is quite respectable.

Kyrgyzstan

With a population of 5.2 million, Kyrgyzstan is the second smallest of the five Central Asian countries.[11] Yet its publishing figures are the healthiest of the five.

Unlike the other four nations, Kyrgyzstan managed, through demonstrations, to throw its authoritarian president out of office and hold a new presidential election, in 2005. Even before then, political conditions were more benign than in Turkmenistan, Tajikistan, and Uzbekistan. For example, an article published in 2000 speaks of the censorship committee having been dissolved. There is also significantly more information to be found about publishing in Kyrgyzstan than in the other four countries, although some of it is apparently inaccurate.[12]

The article from 2000 mentioned above states that there were nearly 30 public and private publishers in the country at that time. An article from 2004 notes that there were then 145 organizations with the right to publish, of which approximately 30 were non-governmental and non-commercial. Publishing statistics for the country can be found in Table 2, with the 1995-98 figures from the United Nations and the later ones directly from the Kyrgyz statistical agency.[13]

Comparing Kyrgyzstan's publication numbers with Tajikistan's (remember that Kyrgyzstan's population is nearly two million less than Tajikistan's), we see that Kyrgyzstan published more than twice as many titles for most of the period under consideration.

Figures for publications from Bishkek appearing in the catalogs of Stanford, LC, and Harvard as of the beginning of August 2006 are shown in Table 3, along with the percent of total publishing output that these figures represent.

As the figures above show, Kyrgyzstan has a healthier publication rate in comparison with the other Central Asian countries, but its overall output is still small. Of course, U.S. libraries are collecting only a small portion of that output (from 11% to 22%). Yet it is likely that the titles received represent most of those of scholarly value.

TABLE 2. Book Publishing in Kyrgyzstan

Item	1995	1996	1998	2000	2001	2002	2003	2004
Books & brochures (printed units)	407	351	420	501	510	672	642	703

TABLE 3. Publications from Bishkek Acquired by Three U.S. Libraries

Library	2001	2002	2003	2004	Total 2001-2004	Percent of Total Publishing Output (2527)
Stanford	72	54	79	63	268	10.6%
Library of Congress	114	128	148	154	544	21.5%
Harvard	132	110	59	37	338	13.4%

CONCLUSION

Most of the 15 to 20 U.S. libraries that collect Central Asian publications feel they are not receiving as many of them as they should be, particularly from Turkmenistan and Tajikistan. However, a review of Stanford's, LC's, and Harvard's online catalog holdings in comparison with publishing data for the region suggests that the main reason libraries are not receiving more titles is that they are not being published.

NOTES

1. The Bibliotechnyi kollektor (Library Collector) was a central Soviet agency that supplied books to libraries within the Soviet Union. It continues to exist in Russia, but is now a private company, currently part of a larger organization called Assotsiatsiia "Sentiabr'." That association also includes a book wholesaler, a seller of office and school supplies, a school of foreign languages, a web design service, etc. The Bibliotechnyi kollektor has a minimal website at http://novric.niac.ru/market/biblio/index.html.

2. Oleg Semikhnenko, e-mail to the author, May 25, 2006.

3. Most of these languages are spoken outside of Central Asia, but the ones listed are Turkic, i.e., related to Uzbek, Kyrgyz, etc.

4. Population figure is from *CIA World Factbook* 2006, http://www.cia.gov/cia/publications/factbook/index.html. "IFLA Protests Closure of Libraries and Violations of Human Rights in Turkmenistan," *IFLA Journal* 31, no. 3:271; Gulnoza Saidazimova, "Central Asia: HRW Highlights Uzbekistan's 'Disastrous' Human Rights Situation," *Radio Free Europe/Radio Liberty*, January 19, 2006, http://www.rferl.org/featuresarticle/2006/1/98C908D2-0C65-4C5F-BAB8-6CD9F1B9D344.html.

5. East View's *CIS & Baltic Periodicals* is one of the subscription databases located at http://dlib.eastview.com/. Articles cited are "Turkmen President Sends his Book *Rukhnama* to Space," *The Times of Central Asia*, 2006, no. 5 (February 3), http://dlib.eastview.com/sources/article.jsp?id=8975175; and TDN, "Turkmenistan–uchastnik

Leiptsigskoi iarmarki," *Neitral'nyi Turkmenistan*, 2004, no. 74 (March 25), http://dlib.eastview.com/sources/article.jsp?id=6153458.

6. CIA World Factbook 2006. For evidence of repression see, for example, Committee to Protect Journalists, "Attacks on the Press in 2005: Europe and Central Asia: Tajikistan," http://www.cpj.org/attacks05/europe05/tajik_05.html; Reporters Sans Frontières, "Tajikistan: 2002 Annual Report," http://www.rsf.org/article.php3?id_article=1791; Reporters Sans Frontières, "Tajikistan: 2006 Annual Report," http://www.rsf.org/article.php3?id_article=17480.

7. *Omori solonai Jumhurii Tojikiston: nashri rasmi = Statisticheskii ezhegodnik Respubliki Tadzhikistan: ofitsial'noe izdanie* (Statistical Yearbook of the Republic of Tajikistan) (Dushanbe: Gos. Komitet statistiki Respubliki Tadzhikistana, 2005), 137.

8. United Nations Statistics Division Common Database, http://unstats.un.org/unsd/cdb/cdb_help/cdb_quick_start.asp. Population data are from the *CIA World Factbook* 2006.

9. Nigora Azimova, e-mail to the author, May 23, 2006. In another e-mail on August 24, 2006, she said the government had shut down both Soros and IREX. Government repression in Uzbekistan is widely documented; see, for example, a large proportion of news stories in the Uzbekistan section on the website of Radio Free Europe/Radio Liberty (http://www.rferl.org/).

10. Igor Cherepanov, "Kazakhstan–Books: First Int'l Book Fair 'Along the Silk Way' Opens in Almaty," *Itar-Tass Weekly News*, April 24, 2001, http://dlib.eastview.com/sources/article.jsp?id=2900619. There is a more detailed description of this fair in Natal'ia Verzhbitskaia, "Knizhnoi iarmarki kraski" (Colors of a Book Fair), *Kazakhstanskaia pravda*, April 28, 2001, http://dlib.eastview.com/sources/article.jsp?id=3289409.

11. *CIA World Factbook* 2006.

12. Zamir Osorov, "Publishing Business in Kyrgyzstan: A Survey," *Times of Central Asia*, August 31, 2000, http://dlib.eastview.com/sources/article.jsp?id=25723. This article claims there were over 1,500 book titles published in 1996, while United Nations statistics have the figure for that year as 351.

13. Osorov, "Publishing Business"; Zh. Togonbaeva and O. Riabov, "K vsemirnomu dniu knigi i avtorskogo prava: bednost' pri izbytke" (To Worldwide Book and Authors' Rights Day: Poverty Amid Abundance), *Slovo Kyrgyzstana*, April 23, 2004, http://dlib.eastview.com/sources/articles.jsp?id=6398384; *United Nations Statistics Division Common Database*; *Kyrgyzstan tsifrlarda=Kyrgyzstan v tsifrakh* (Kyrgyzstan in Figures) (Bishkek: Kyrgyz Respublikasynyn Uluttuk statistika komiteti, 2005), 275. *Kyrgyzstan tsifrlarda* claims that the numbers represent thousands, but that is impossible. The publishing output for all of Russia in 2004, for example, was slightly more than 89,000 titles. See Kristine Bushnell and John Bushnell, "Publishing Thrives While the Government Tightens Control Over the Media: A Report to Slavic Librarians, June 2005," *Slavic & East European Information Resources* 7, no. 1 (2006), 84.

doi:10.1300/J167v08n02_04

APPENDIX 1. Survey Questions

Please answer only if your library collects material published in these countries: Kazakhstan, Kyrgyzstan, Tajikistan, Turkmenistan, Uzbekistan. Send your answers to me at rondest@stanford.edu; I'll collate them and report back to the list.

1. Which of these countries does your library collect publications from?
2. In what languages does your library collect publications from these countries? Russian and/or Western languages only, or also in the vernaculars?
3. In what subjects does your library collect from these countries?
4. Who at your library handles collection development from these countries, the person responsible for Slavic material, the person responsible for Middle Eastern material, or someone else? If you are not that person, please include his or her name and e-mail address or pass this message to him/her.
5. Is one of these countries more problematic for your library than the others? Which one?
6. Would your library potentially be interested in participating in a cooperative acquisition program with LC? (The publications would not be free.)
7. Can your library's acquisitions operation handle methods of acquiring material that do not involve purchase from a vendor?

APPENDIX 2. Summary of U.S. Libraries' Collecting of Central Asian Publications. From Survey Results, Updates by Survey Participants in May 2006, and LC's Website

Institution	Countries collected from	Languages collected	Subjects collected	Collection development done by	Most problematic country
Columbia University	All 5	Russian, Western, all vernaculars including minority lgs.	Full profile of humanities & social sciences, including belles lettres	Slavic librarian	Tajikistan
Duke University	All 5	Only Russian & Western languages	Broad profile of social sciences & humanities	Slavic librarian	All are problematic, but Turkmenistan, as the most closed society, probably most difficult
Harvard	All 5	Russian & vernaculars; Middle East has approval plan with ATC	Social sciences & humanities, but no music, art or anthropology	Russian & Western lgs.: Slavic librarian. Vernaculars: Middle East librarian	Tajikistan, Turkmenistan
Hoover Institution (see also Stanford University)	All 5	Russian, Western & vernaculars	Until Sept. 2001, recent history; social sciences, archival material. Since Sept. 2001, archival material	Slavic librarian	
Indiana University	All 5	Russian, Western, Turkic	Social sciences & humanities	Russian & Western lngs: Slavic librarian. Vernaculars: Middle East librarian	
Library of Congress	All 5	Russian, Western, vernaculars	Full profile of humanities & social sciences, including belles lettres	Middle East librarians	

APPENDIX 2. (continued)

Institution	Countries	Languages	Subjects	Cataloger	Problem areas
New York Public Library	All 5	Emphasis on vernaculars; Russian & Western languages acquired selectively	Social sciences & humanities	Middle East librarian	
Stanford University	All 5	Russian, Western; vernaculars	Emphasis on political science, history, statistics	Slavic librarian	Turkmenistan, Tajikistan
University of California, Berkeley	All 5, selectively	Russian if possible, but vernacular for literature and language, folklore, etc., where having it in the original language is important	Most social sciences & humanities	Slavic librarian	"No, dealers like ATC and Krieger seem to make available enough materials to satisfy our needs."
University of Chicago	All 5	All languages	All areas of humanities & social sciences	Slavic librarian	None
University of Illinois, Urbana-Champaign	All 5	Russian & Western languages; literature in vernaculars	Social sciences & humanities; large collection of newspapers	Slavic librarians	Turkmenistan is most problematic, followed by Tajikistan
University of Iowa	Kazakhstan, mostly	Selectively in Russian	Political science, history, ethnic relations	Slavic librarian	
University of Kansas	All 5	Social sciences in Russian & Western languages; language, culture, folklore in vernaculars	Social sciences & humanities (evidently not literature)	Russian & Western lgs: Slavic librarian. Vernaculars: Slavc Serials Cataloger, who also knows other lgs.	

University of Michigan	All 5	All languages	Social sciences and humanities, with some collection of math and the sciences (including ecology)	Slavic librarian	Kyrgyzstan is problematic because it is so impoverished. Turkmenistan is problematic because of its politics.
University of North Carolina, Chapel Hill	All 5	Russian, Western; will probably consider major publications in vernacular	Literature, literary criticism, folklore, history, sociology	Slavic librarian	All of them are equally problematic
University of Texas, Austin	All 5, selectively	Tajikistan (and Azerbaijan) selectively in vernacular; others selectively in English; occasionally also in Russian	Social sciences & humanities	Russian & Western lgs.: Slavic librarian; Vernaculars: Middle East librarian	All of them are equally problematic; says not easily available from vendors
University of Washington	All, but very little from Tajikistan and sporadically from Turkmenistan	Russian, Western, all vernaculars	Language, literature, history, politics, social sciences	Russian & Western: Slavic librarian. Vernaculars: Middle East librarian	Turkmenistan, then Tajikistan
University of Wisconsin - Madison	All 5	All languages	History, literature, linguistics, political science, economics	Slavic librarian	Tajikistan

Modern Greek Collections at U.S. Libraries: New Directions

Harold M. Leich

SUMMARY. The author describes events, meetings, conferences, and plans since 1999 for increasing communication and cooperation among librarians at American academic and research libraries that support Modern Greek collections. Events and groups discussed include the 1999 Library of Congress conference, Strengthening Modern Greek Collections; the Library Committee of the Modern Greek Studies Association; and the Consortium of Hellenic Studies Librarians. doi:10.1300/J167v08n02_05 *[Article copies available for a fee from The Haworth Document Delivery Service: 1-800-HAWORTH. E-mail address: <docdelivery@haworthpress.com> Website: <http://www.HaworthPress.com> © 2007 by The Haworth Press, Inc. All rights reserved.]*

KEYWORDS. Modern Greek collections, Hellenic collections, Library of Congress, Modern Greek Studies Association, Consortium of Hellenic Studies Librarians, United States, libraries

---

Harold M. Leich, MA, MLS, is Russian Area Specialist, European Division, Library of Congress, Washington, DC 20540-4830 USA (E-mail: hlei@loc.gov).

The author would like to express his gratitude to Phoebe Peacock, Angela Cannon, and Rhea Karabelas Lesage for comments and input on this article. Opinions expressed herein are those of the author and not of the Library of Congress or the United States government.

[Haworth co-indexing entry note]: "Modern Greek Collections at U.S. Libraries: New Directions." Leich, Harold M. Co-published simultaneously in *Slavic & East European Information Resources* (The Haworth Information Press, an imprint of The Haworth Press, Inc.) Vol. 8, No. 2/3, 2007, pp. 49-54; and: *Access to East European and Eurasian Culture: Publishing, Acquisitions, Digitization, Metadata* (ed: Miranda Remnek) The Haworth Information Press, an imprint of The Haworth Press, Inc., 2007, pp. 49-54. Single or multiple copies of this article are available for a fee from The Haworth Document Delivery Service [1-800- HAWORTH, 9:00 a.m. - 5:00 p.m. (EST). E-mail address: docdelivery@haworthpress.com].

Available online at http://seeir.haworthpress.com
doi:10.1300/J167v08n02_05

Greece (Modern Greece, that is, post-1453 and especially post-independence, contemporary Greece) is something of an "orphaned" country when it comes to how American libraries traditionally divide the world to provide coverage of foreign countries and languages in support of area studies programs.[1] While located geographically in the eastern part of Europe, and in the Balkans, Greece was nevertheless–during the large build-up of library area studies programs during the Cold War period–*not* part of the Soviet bloc, but rather a NATO member, an important member of the Western alliance, and an integral part of the non-communist world.[2] In addition, Greece has always been considered one of the most important sources of our own "Western civilization," however that is defined. For these reasons and probably a number of others, Greece is not ordinarily handled by "Slavic and East European" librarians and library collections at American libraries, but rather by Classics librarians, Western European specialists or, sadly, not at all.[3] One ironic result of this is that the Eastern European but non-Slavic countries that *were* part of the Soviet bloc (e.g., Hungary, Romania, Albania, and the Baltic states) have received much more comprehensive attention at American research libraries, and better funding for collection building, than has Greece.

It has been only in the past few years that librarians and information specialists involved with Modern Greek collections at American libraries have begun to organize, to get to know each other and each other's collections, to share their professional experiences, and to plan cooperative action to improve access to Modern Greek materials.[4] Slavic and East European librarians, on the other hand, can trace their collective collaborative efforts back to conferences in the 1960s and 1970s, particularly the Slavic Librarians' Conference held at the University of Illinois at Urbana-Champaign in September 1975.[5]

In the case of Greece, it was not until 1999 that a conference of librarians involved in Greek studies was actually held at the Library of Congress (LC)[6]–even though bibliographers and librarians at the several Modern Greek collections in the U.S. had previously maintained informal and occasional contact with each other. But the 1999 conference was also attended by a number of librarians from Greece, a fitting culmination to years of planning and fundraising by David H. Kraus (1923-1997), Assistant Chief of LC's European Division. Kraus also functioned for twenty years, 1977-1997, as LC's *de facto* Modern Greek specialist and bibliographer. In addition to his numerous administrative duties, Kraus handled selection of Greek monographs and serials, and with great enthusiasm answered incoming Greek reference questions, including many from the Congress. His untimely death in 1997 meant that he could not actually attend the conference he had worked on planning for so many years.[7]

There was very little follow-up to the 1999 conference, and for a variety of reasons. Some of the Greek libraries represented did not yet have reliable e-mail access, so communication was therefore a problem. In addition, by pure chance there was a major generational change in the early 2000s–many of the people present at the 1999 conference, both Greeks and Americans, retired over the next few years. A Library Committee was formed in the U.S. within the Modern Greek Studies Association (MGSA), and there were small meetings of this group at several MGSA conferences.[8] However, none of the working groups established at the 1999 LC conference really functioned as such in the years after the conference.

In November 2004, an informal group of librarians involved with Greek collections from all periods (Classical, Byzantine, and Modern) met at Harvard University's Center for Hellenic Studies in Washington, DC to discuss topics of mutual interest.[9] The participants agreed that a more permanent arrangement of some sort, with broader participation, was needed to facilitate the exchange of information and ideas among American librarians involved with Greek collections. Another important goal of the discussions was the expansion of contacts with colleagues in Western Europe and Greece itself. The result of the November 2004 meetings was the formation of a group eventually named the Consortium of Hellenic Studies Librarians (CoHSL),[10] currently under the leadership of Rebecka Lindau of Princeton University. While many of the participants in the consortium are involved primarily with Modern Greek collections, the group also includes librarians and bibliographers at collections of Classical and Byzantine-era Greek materials.

The 2005 conference of the Modern Greek Studies Association in Chicago had, as part of its program for the first time, a formal panel on Greek library- and archives-related issues. Held on November 5, 2005, the panel contained eight presentations on various aspects of Greek collections. Deborah Brown (Dumbarton Oaks, Washington, DC) described her Byzantine collections and the opening of a new library facility in September, 2005. Jacqueline Riley (University of Cincinnati) discussed her university's substantial Classics and Modern Greek collections, and distributed lists of Cincinnati's pre-1900 Greek newspapers and periodicals. George Zachos (University of Ioannina Library), formerly director of the National Library of Greece, gave a report on conditions at the National Library and its bibliographic products and services.

Maria Pantelia (University of California, Irvine) reported on the *Thesaurus Linguae Graecae*, the aim of which is to record every Greek word ever put into writing, from Homer until 1900. With over 1.3 million unique words already included, this digital project will also include the full texts of all known Greek writings. George Paganelis (California State University, Sacramento) described the Tsakopoulos Collection, one of the largest Modern Greek print and archival collections in the U.S., and in addition discussed the need for an index (analogous to the *American Bibliography of Slavic and East European Studies*) oriented to Modern Greek studies, which would include articles from a wide variety of American, Greek, and foreign periodicals. Rhea Karabelas Lesage (Harvard University) reported on a proposal made by LC's Cataloging Policy and Support Office (CPSO) in summer 2004 to change LC romanization for Modern Greek, and the CoHSL's effort to delay this decision until the impact of such a change could be analyzed by the library community. In the end, CPSO decided to delay the changes to a future date.

Maria Georgopoulou (Gennadius Library, Athens) gave a report on her library, part of the American School of Classical Studies in Athens. It is one of the largest collections of Modern Greek publications in the world, and maintains manuscript and archival holdings as well. Finally, this author (Harold Leich, LC) discusssed a project in process to compile a directory for American scholars describing the Modern Greek archival system and providing bibliographic citations for published descriptions, catalogs, and finding aids for manuscript materials in that system.

In addition to the formal panel discussion, the MGSA Library Committee held its business meeting on November 5. The event included a presentation by staff from the Center for Research Libraries (CRL), Chicago, on the Global Resources Network coordinated by and based at CRL. There are currently resource projects for Germany, Latin America, France, and several other areas.[11] The CoHSL organizers had invited CRL in order to stimulate interest in establishing such a project for Greece.

Following up on the idea for a Modern Greek resources project, an all-day meeting was held at Widener Library at Harvard University on February 22, 2006, with CRL and several major Modern Greek collections represented (Harvard; Yale; LC; California State, Sacramento; and the Gennadius Library, Athens). The conclusion reached at the meeting was to proceed on establishing a Modern Greek Resources Project, with the following priorities:

1. Reformatting (microfilming and digitization) as a means of preservation as well as of acquisition;
2. Bibliographic control (more comprehensive and timelier provision of full bibliographic data to American libraries; training of Greek librarians in cataloging standards);
3. Resource sharing and document delivery;
4. An index of Greek periodicals.

It was also agreed that the American librarians would meet with representatives from Greek libraries in Athens in December 2006.

The past decade, and particularly the past few years, 2004-2006, have been very productive for American librarians handling Modern Greek collections. Reasons of economy and efficiency make it imperative to improve communication and to develop more collaborative projects, in areas such as exchange of bibliographic data, acquisitions, digitization, resource sharing and document delivery, to meet what are expected to be increased demands for access to Modern Greek materials in the future. These demands are likely to stem from a perceptible trend among centers of Slavic and East European Studies nationwide–such as that at the University of Illinois–to expand their sphere of coverage actively as the dimensions of Slavic area studies change. Indeed, new geopolitical realities are promoting greater emphasis not only on the liberated countries of the former Soviet Union in the Caucasus and Central Asia, but also on the more traditional countries of Southeast Europe, Bulgaria, Romania and the Former Yugoslavia. But countries such as Greece and Turkey, which were usually considered outside the Slavic and East European sphere, are now of greatly increased interest, and emerging programs on these areas are bound to create a new demand for materials that efforts like those described in this article will surely help to satisfy.[12]

NOTES

1. Cyprus, Finland, and Mongolia, for different reasons, are also "orphans" in many American library area studies programs, if indeed they are covered at all. The Greek-speaking part of Cyprus is included in the scope of this article.

2. An important and influential report by the Association of Research Libraries (ARL) explicitly places Greece in Western Europe when it discusses library collections

at U.S. libraries: Jutta Reed-Scott, *Scholarship, Research Libraries, and Global Publishing* (Washington, DC: ARL, 1996), 111.

3. It should be noted that at a few American libraries, e.g., the University of Chicago, University of Michigan, and University of Minnesota, Modern Greece has been handled, and quite ably, by the Slavic and East European bibliographer.

4. There are roughly fifteen to twenty U.S. libraries with major Modern Greek collections, including the following: Harvard University; Yale University; University of Cincinnati; University of Chicago; Center for Research Libraries; University of Michigan; University of Minnesota; Ohio State University; Columbia University; New York University; New York Public Library; Princeton University; Library of Congress; Dumbarton Oaks; University of California, Berkeley; and California State University, Sacramento.

5. The Slavic Librarians' Conference was held September 11-13, 1975, in Urbana, Illinois and did not include Greece. Conferences in the 1960s included the Conference on Bibliographic and Research Aids in Soviet Studies held at Columbia University's Greyston Conference Center, Riverdale, New York, November 19-22, 1966. Source: personal recollections of the author (for the 1975 conference); uncataloged archival materials from both conferences in the European Division, Library of Congress.

6. Materials and papers from the April 1999 conference, "Strengthening Modern Greek Collections: Building U.S.-Greek Library Partnerships," are available online: http://www.loc.gov/rr/european/GrkColl/GrkConf.html (September 30, 2006).

7. Basic biographical information is available in Kraus's obituary, *The Washington Post*, November 1, 1997, p. B6.

8. For example, the MGSA conference held November 1999 at Princeton University. Information about the association is available at its website: http://www.mgsa.org/.

9. Institutions represented, besides the Center itself, included Dumbarton Oaks, Yale University, Harvard University, Princeton University, New York University, Columbia University, and the Library of Congress. The Center's website is available at: http://www.chs.harvard.edu/.

10. The consortium's website is available at: http://www.cohsl.net/.

11. Information on the Global Resources Network is available at the project's home page: http://www.crl.edu/grn/index.asp. An overview of all CRL programs is available at its home page: http://www.crl.edu/.

12. For evidence of these trends, readers may consult various recent articles in *Newsnet: News of the American Association for the Advancement of Slavic Studies*. See for example: Katherine Verdery, "What's in a Name and Should We Change Ours?" *Newsnet* 46, no. 2 (2006): 1-4; Ronald Suny and Dmitry Gorenburg, "Where Are We Going? What Is to Be Done?," *Newsnet* 46, no. 4 (2006): 1-4.

doi:10.1300/J167v08n02_05

Acquisitions Problems in Ukrainian Libraries and New Electronic Solutions

Olena Bashun

SUMMARY. The author discusses a wide range of new developments in Ukrainian libraries that affects library acquisitions. New strategies are now required for obtaining library materials due to the inadequacy of obligatory deposit and changes in bibliographic control of new publications. Libraries are actively developing computer and Internet technologies, including websites, online catalogs, access to databases, sites linking to online resources, and collections of digitized full-text material. A number of libraries have recently begun implementing virtual reference services. A new professional journal, whose title translates as *Library Forum of Ukraine*, has arisen to address all aspects of librarianship. doi:10.1300/J167v08n02_06 *[Article copies available for a fee from The Haworth Document Delivery Service: 1-800-HAWORTH. E-mail address: <docdelivery@haworthpress.com> Website: <http://www.HaworthPress.com> © 2007 by The Haworth Press, Inc. All rights reserved.]*

Olena Bashun, PhD, is Vice Director, Donetsk Regional Universal Scientific Library, Artema St. 84, Donetsk, Ukraine, 83055; and Head, Donetsk Regional Department of the Ukrainian Library Association (E-mail: olena@library.donetsk.ua).

[Haworth co-indexing entry note]: "Acquisitions Problems in Ukrainian Libraries and New Electronic Solutions." Bashun, Olena. Co-published simultaneously in *Slavic & East European Information Resources* (The Haworth Information Press, an imprint of The Haworth Press, Inc.) Vol. 8, No. 2/3, 2007, pp. 55-69; and: *Access to East European and Eurasian Culture: Publishing, Acquisitions, Digitization, Metadata* (ed: Miranda Remnek) The Haworth Information Press, an imprint of The Haworth Press, Inc., 2007, pp. 55-69. Single or multiple copies of this article are available for a fee from The Haworth Document Delivery Service [1-800-HAWORTH, 9:00 a.m. - 5:00 p.m. (EST). E-mail address: docdelivery@haworthpress.com].

Available online at http://seeir.haworthpress.com
© 2007 by The Haworth Press, Inc. All rights reserved.
doi:10.1300/J167v08n02_06

KEYWORDS. Ukraine, Ukrainian, library, libraries, acquisition, obligatory deposit, bibliographic control, electronic resources, technology, virtual reference service

INTRODUCTION

The main function of a library is to provide its readers with exhaustive information. In this age of electronic and computer technologies, the transformation process in libraries has as one of its goals an expansion in the use of electronic technologies. Ukrainian libraries are gradually adopting electronic technologies alongside traditional ones.

The Ukrainian library system consists of approximately 45,000 libraries, including four national libraries, four state libraries, over 18,000 public libraries belonging to the system of the Ministry of Culture and Tourism of Ukraine, 97 libraries of the National Academy of Sciences, 193 libraries that are part of institutions of higher education, over 1,000 medical libraries, and over 22,000 school libraries. Total holdings equal approximately 700 million volumes. Ukrainian libraries serve about 25 million readers, to whom they lend over 500 million books per year. A total of 70,000 librarians are employed in these libraries.

LIBRARY ACQUISITIONS AND BIBLIOGRAPHIC CONTROL OF NEW UKRAINIAN PUBLICATIONS

Acquisition of library materials is a very important activity for providing readers with new information. The following methods of acquisition are used by the libraries of Ukraine:

- Traditional (purchasing books, periodicals, and other printed materials)
- Electronic (purchasing electronic books and periodicals; providing access to free electronic resources; creating the library's own electronic resources; and transforming print resources into electronic versions)

In order for libraries to acquire appropriate material, it is necessary to have information about what is being published in Ukraine. Attempts have been made to create a Ukrainian equivalent of *Books in Print*, but all of them were unsuccessful. There is at present no reliable information about books being prepared for publication, a situation that hampers the work of libraries and causes considerable problems in acquiring them.

The Book Chamber of Ukraine registers all printed production in the country by publishing the periodicals *Litopys knyh* (Chronicle of Books), *Litopys hazetnykh statei* (Chronicle of Newspaper Articles), *Litopys zhurnal'nykh statei* (Chronicle of Journal Articles), *Litopys avtoreferativ dysertatsii* (Chronicle of Dissertation Abstracts), *Litopys not* (Chronicle of Music Scores), etc. However, this information appears only after the material is published–by which time some of it has already disappeared from the book market. The registration function is based on the principle of obligatory deposit, but practice proves that not all publishing houses observe the Law on Obligatory Copy (Obligatory or Legal Deposit). A contributing factor to this non-compliance is the absence of sanctions. These factors cause information about the publication output of the country to be incomplete.

To our great regret, the Book Chamber of Ukraine's website (http://www.ukrbook.net/) provides only information about its services. Electronic access to its *Litopysy* requires payment through the company East View Information Services (http://www.eastview.com/). Information about forthcoming and already-published books must be drawn from periodicals whose purpose is to advertise them.

There are a number of such periodicals, many of which have both print and online versions. One example is *Knyzhnyk-review*, a newspaper published both in print and electronic versions (http://www.review.kiev.ua/); it gives information about news and events in the Ukrainian book trade, and includes reviews and summaries of new books and ratings of bestsellers. It also holds the competitions Chudesna semertsa (Wonderful Seven) and Knyha roku (Book of the Year), as well as selling books by mail (Knyha poshtoi). *Druh chytacha* (Friend of the Reader), a print newspaper, gives information about the book market and reviews new books; it has no website. The journal and website *Knyzhkovyi klub* (Book Club) functions both as a journal and Internet shop (http://www.bookclub.ua/ukr/club/; Russian version: http://www.bookclub.ua/), providing information about books available for sale, collected works, and collector's editions and gift editions; it also announces new books. The journal *Knyzhkovyi ohliad* (Book Review) has print and electronic versions (http://www.web-standart.net/magaz.php?sid = 6). It gives information about new publications and analysis of the book market. An electronic archive of the journal is available for the period 2001-2004. The newspaper *Krytyka* (Criticism) also has print and electronic versions (http://www.krytyka.kiev.ua/). It publishes book reviews and gives analyses of the book market. The journal *Bibliotechnyi forum Ukrainy* (Library Forum of Ukraine) has print and electronic versions (electronic version available through http://www.idea.com.ua/); it presents news related to libraries and library and information science.

Information about new books can also be obtained through the book-search website *Knyzhkovyi kur'ier* (Book Courier, http://www.book-courier.com.ua/). It lists new books classified according to subject, furnished by the National Parliamentary Library of Ukraine. It also has links to institutions and events selling books, including publishing houses, stores, and book fairs; as well as retrospective information about books published in Ukraine since 1995. But despite the availability of these periodicals and websites, and the details they provide, the uncoordinated nature of information about publications in the country complicates the acquisition process in libraries.

LIBRARY ACQUISITIONS AND OBLIGATORY DEPOSIT

The primary acquisition source for published materials in Ukrainian libraries has long been obligatory deposit copies, which the law stipulates they should receive. National and state libraries should receive free deposit copies of material published throughout the country. Regional libraries should receive free deposit copies of materials published in their regions. However, the system of obligatory deposit functions poorly. In 2006, the Donetsk Regional General Scientific Library conducted a study on receipt of obligatory deposit copies during the last five years by libraries listed in the law as recipients. The data show that the libraries studied did not receive obligatory deposit copies of as many as fifty to seventy percent of the books registered in *Litopys knyh*.

To improve the performance of obligatory deposit, it is necessary to change the law by holding publishers responsible for not providing obligatory deposit copies. Librarians and representatives of the Ministry of Culture and Tourism have held an all-Ukrainian discussion on this problem.

LIBRARY ACQUISITION BY PURCHASE

Ukrainian libraries now acquire books and serials primarily by purchasing them from subscription agencies and book-trading firms.

Subscription Agencies

There are more than 100 subscription agencies in Ukraine, the largest of which will be discussed here. The state periodical distribution enterprise Presa publishes subscription catalogs in printed form. It also has a website (http://www.presaukr.kiev.ua/), with catalogs of periodicals, and it sells books on subscription.

The research and production company Idea (http://www.idea.com.ua/) has a subscription agency that specializes in serving libraries and enterprises. It has operated for more than 10 years, providing materials to over 900 libraries in Ukraine and Russia, with branch offices all over Ukraine. The firm publishes catalogs of Ukrainian periodicals (over 2,000 titles), Russian periodicals (over 6,000 titles), and foreign periodicals (over 6,300 titles). Print-format catalogs are sent to libraries; electronic versions are available on the company's website. Clients can place subscriptions and register them on the website; issues are delivered through the firm's network of branch offices around the country. The company provides invoices to libraries, including a listing of journals and their prices. Invoices can be supplied in electronic format and put into the registration card index in the library. Clients can check the performance of their subscriptions on the website. The majority of Ukrainian libraries, from the largest to the smallest, use the Idea agency as the result of competitive bidding. The company also serves foreign clients, and it welcomes new library subscriptions from abroad.

The subscription agency Tsentr navchal'noi literatury (Center for Educational Literature, also known as Periodica) publishes subscription catalogs of periodicals for Ukraine, Russia, and foreign countries in print and electronic formats. Its website can be found at http://www.periodica.com.ua/; it serves libraries.

The subscription agency Sammit, Ltd., has about 10,000 subscribers in Kiev and 40,000 in the regions of Ukraine. It works with institutions and individuals. Its website is located at http://www.summit.ua/.

The information agency K.I.S.S., Ltd., publishes subscription catalogs (5,000 periodical titles), and has a network of offices throughout Ukraine. Subscriptions can be placed through the firm's website, http://www.kiss.kiev.ua/). Ninety percent of its clients are institutions and five percent are individuals.

Book-Trading Firms

Among suppliers of monographs working with libraries, the largest is the research and production company Idea (http://www.idea.com.ua/).

The monograph vendor arm of this supplier to libraries and other institutions (as well as to individuals) has a network of bookstores throughout Ukraine as well as an Internet bookstore on its website. It publishes catalogs of books from Ukraine (over 30,000 titles) and Russia (80,000 titles) in printed and electronic formats. Clients can place orders on the site, find information on books and periodicals, and purchase books in the Internet bookstore. Selection of books can be accomplished by subject, author, title, year of publication, publishing house, etc.; orders are delivered through its network of branch offices. One can subscribe to regular lists of new books by e-mail. A program called Tender has been developed for facilitating competitive bidding and comparing price lists; it can be used at the site free of charge. Clients can check on their orders by entering the Idea site and checking the data (every client has his/her password allowing entry). As mentioned earlier, this firm also serves foreign clients, and welcomes subscriptions from abroad.

Libraries also acquire books from bookstores, the majority of which have websites. Some of these are Bambuk (Bambook), http://www.bambook.com/; Folio, http://bookpost.com.ua/; On-Line BookStore, formerly at http://www.books.com.ua/, now taken over by the publisher Znannia, http://www.znannia.com.ua/; DiaMail Book Internet Store, http://www.diamail.kiev.ua/; and Bookshop, http://bookshop.kiev.ua/. These stores present plans of publishing houses, as well as newly received books, book ratings, and news of the book trade. Libraries can order books quickly and receive invoices for payment. Actual payment can be made using cash, cashless settlement, payment on delivery, or electronic payment. The Internet stores hold such marketing events as lotteries, drawing of prizes, and competitions.

Another source for acquisition is Ukrainian publishers (about 700 of them are registered in the country). The development of the Internet has allowed many of them to create websites and sell books through them. Some examples are Yurincom Inter, http://www.yurincom.kiev.ua/books; Kal'variia, http://www.calvaria.org/; Sofiia, http://sofia.com.ua/; Akta, http://www.acta.com.ua/; Svit (Light), http://www.dsv-svit.lviv.ua/; Svichado, http://www.svichado.com/; Lybid, http://www.lybid.org.ua; Publishing House Nautilus, http://www.nautilus.com.ua/; Zvukovaia kniga (Audio Book), http://www.audiobook.com.ua/. The list of such publishers could be continued, as their number is constantly increasing in virtual space. Acquiring books from publishers directly is not advantageous for libraries, however, because they are interested in wholesale purchases. Even so, publishing houses' websites are useful for acquainting librarians with newly published literature.

Competitive Bidding Requirement

The acquisition process in Ukrainian libraries is considerably complicated by laws in force requiring libraries to purchase only on the basis of competitive bids if the sum is higher than 30,000 hrivnas ($6,242 on December 21, 2006). Librarians lobbied strenuously for revocation of the Tender Law during an all-Ukrainian meeting held on the initiative of the Ukrainian Library Association, in which the representatives from the Ministry of Economy and the Ministry of Culture and Tourism also took part.

UKRAINIAN LIBRARIES AND THEIR ELECTRONIC RESOURCES

Electronic resources supplement traditional print resources. The libraries of Ukraine are actively developing computer and Internet technologies. Over 150 libraries have websites, with fifty-two percent of them providing electronic catalogs. Sixty-three percent of those are research libraries and seventy-eight percent are libraries of educational institutions.

The U.S. Department of State provided considerable assistance in the development of Internet technologies. One hundred eight Internet centers with free access were opened in the framework of the LEAP Project, as well as 22 Window on America Centers supported by the U.S. Embassy in Ukraine and 24 IATP (Internet Access and Training Program) Centers.

Development of electronic resources in Ukrainian libraries is occurring in the following areas: creating bibliographic databases (online book catalogs), providing access to existing databases (free and paid), creating electronic libraries (aggregating existing full-text documents and performing original conversion of print documents to electronic format), and establishing virtual reference services.

Libraries Presenting Bibliographic Information in Electronic Catalogs

National Libraries

V. Vernads'kyi National Library of Ukraine (http://www.nbuv.gov.ua/portal/libukr.html).
- Catalog with 346,000 bibliographic descriptions
- Specialized catalogs and indexes
- Catalog of dissertations and dissertation abstracts (45,000 bibliographic descriptions of dissertations, 60,000 descriptions of dissertation abstracts)
- Catalog of periodicals (15,500 bibliographic descriptions of journals and other continuing publications)
- Bibliographic database of collection of presidents of Ukraine (19,500 bibliographic descriptions)
- Index of publications from 1980 to 1999 (930,000 bibliographic descriptions of publications of the USSR and Ukraine)
- Index of translations from 1980 to 2001 (1,300,000 bibliographic descriptions of books from different countries and peoples translated into over 100 languages)
- Index of journal articles in the reading room (40,000 bibliographic descriptions on social and economic subjects, materials acquired in the years 1995-2002)
- Website linking to the sites of other libraries in Ukraine and around the world, structured according to type of library

National Parliamentary Library of Ukraine (NPLU) (http://www.nplu.org/)

- Catalog of books and special editions (120,559 entries)
- Index of dissertation abstracts (52,957 entries)
- Index of articles in scholarly collections (278,595 entries)
- Catalog of journals (7,306 titles)
- Catalog of newspapers (685 titles)
- Index *Policy and Politicians as Reflected in Periodicals of Ukraine* (over 30,000 entries)
- Multi-subject database of periodical articles (over 22,000 entries)
- Website linking to state, regional, city, and district libraries, with those providing access to electronic catalogs specially marked

National Scientific Medical Library (http://www.library.gov.ua/)

- Database of Ukrainian and foreign books and abstracts. Includes records for books (monographs, yearbooks, collections of articles, proceedings of conferences and other events, dissertation abstracts) in medicine, public health, pedagogy, psychology, biology, chemistry, physics, biotechnology, physical culture, labor protection, ecology, culture, social sciences in general, branch patents, and inventions. Codes and commentaries given alongside bibliographic descriptions. Database partially annotated.
- Registration and analytical database of Ukrainian and foreign periodicals reflecting acquisitions from 1995 to date. Contains analytical descriptions of selected journal articles in medicine, public health, pedagogy, psychology, chemistry, biology, biotechnology, physical culture, ecology, labor protection, branch patents, and inventions.
- Bibliographic database of patent descriptions for Ukrainian inventions.

National Library for Children (http://www.chl.kiev.ua/)

- Electronic catalog, but number of entries not indicated

State Libraries

Korolenko Kharkiv State Research Library (http://korolenko.kharkov.com)

- Electronic catalog includes 130,000 bibliographic records

M. Gor'kii Odessa State Scientific Library (http://www.ognb.odessa.ua/)

- Electronic catalog includes 66,670 bibliographic records and 500,000 articles

Regional Libraries

Among regional libraries, nine have electronic catalogs. Kirovograd, Donetsk, Kherson, and Dnepropetrovsk regional scientific libraries are the leaders in the number of bibliographic records. Their websites can be found through the National Parliamentary Library of Ukraine (http://profy.nplu.org/library/index.htm).

Libraries of Institutions of Higher Education

The majority of libraries of institutions of higher education have electronic catalogs. The largest are: Research Library of the T. Shevchenko National University (over 750, 000 bibliographic records); Scientific-Technical Library of the Kiev Polytechnic National University of Ukraine (http://library.ntu-kpi.kiev.ua/); Research Library of the V. Karazin Kharkov National University (http://www-library.univer.kharkov.ua/); and Research Library of the Kyiv-Mohyla Academy National University (http://www.library.ukma.kiev.ua/).

Special Libraries

Few special libraries have electronic catalogs. One exception is the State Scientific Technical Library of Ukraine (http://www.gntb.n-t.org/); the number of records is not given. It also has other databases:

- *Foreign Scientific and Technical Journal Subscriptions in Ukrainian Libraries for the Current Year*
- Reference database *Deposited Research Reports*
- Database of patents and legal literature
- Database *Standards of Ukraine*

Electronic catalogs of other special libraries can be reached through the site of the V. Vernads'kyi National Library of Ukraine (http://www.nbuv.gov.ua/portal/libukr.html).

A new website, *Bibliotechnyi informatsiinyi portal* (Bibliographic Information Portal, http://www.librportal.org.ua), facilitates access to library-based web resources.

Electronic Resources Provided Through Consortia

Unfortunately, in Ukraine there is as yet no cooperative database that would allow simultaneous searching of library holdings, such as *WorldCat* in the United States, or in Russia the LIBNET Center (http://www.nilc.ru/) and the ARBICON consortium (http://www.arbicon.ru/). However, a new trend in Ukrainian libraries is purchasing and providing access to databases, both paid and free. Libraries took the initial step in providing access to full-text databases in the late 1990s, with 400 journals from the publisher Springer, assisted by George Soros's International Renaissance Foundation. Beginning in 2002 and lasting through 2007, a project called Access to Electronic Journals for Researchers of Ukraine, has been running in libraries, part of the INASP program (Access to Scientific Publications; see http://www.intas.be/index.asp?s= 20&uid). This program is run by INTAS (International Association for the Promotion of Cooperation with Scientists from the New Independent States of the Former Soviet Union, an EU organization) under a grant provided by the National Scientific and Technical Library of Germany and the University Library of Hanover. The Ukrainian coordinator for the project is the Research Library of the Kyiv-Mohyla Academy National University. Two hundred fifty-two libraries in the country participate. The program provides free access to the SpringerLink online journal collection (http://www.springerlink.com/), which includes over 1,200 peer-reviewed journals (over 600,000 documents) in science, technology, and medicine, with an archive available beginning in 1996; to the Blackwell Collection of Online Journals (approximately 330 journals in science, technology, and medicine; see http://www.black wellpublishing.com/cservices/journal_online.asp); to various other electronic journals via the Internet (full texts of articles in 9,691 journals); to Zentralblatt Mathemetik (a bibliographic database in mathematics with approximately 1.9 million abstracts from 2,300 journals and other serials); and to TIBORDER (electronic document delivery).

In 2003, the association Informatio-Consortium was founded for the purpose of implementing the project Electronic Information for Libraries–eIFL Direct (Electronic Information For Libraries, http://www.eifl.net/), being a joint initiative of the Open Society Institute in Budapest and EBSCO Publishing. The project provides access to full-text databases from EBSCO, ProQuest, BIOone, Cambridge University Press, Oxford University Press, Gale Publishing Group, Sage Publishing, American Physical Association Publishing, Institute of Physics Publishing, Elsevier, STN International, East View Information Services, Springer, Kluwer and Blackwell Publishing, Integrum-Techno, and Rubrikon (the last two being databases in Russian). Over fifty Ukrainian libraries participate in this project. Access to the databases is provided at minimal cost.

The Journal Donation Project, based in New York, gives Ukrainian libraries the opportunity to receive American periodicals in the humanities in either print or electronic format.

Electronic Resources Created by Ukrainian Libraries

In addition to purchasing existing databases, the libraries of Ukraine also create their own full-text electronic resources. General tendencies in the development of electronic libraries are as follows:
- Mounting electronic versions of documents and making them freely available, either with the author's consent or after they have passed into the public domain;
- Mounting digitized publications of the library itself (methodological, bibliographic) and making them freely available;
- Providing access to materials via the Internet onsite in the library only (typical especially for libraries of institutions of higher education);
- Providing links to full-text online resources available over the Internet;
- Digitizing print publications–while observing copyright requirements.

Largest Freely-Available Full-Text Electronic Collections in Ukrainian Libraries

V. Vernads'kyi National Library of Ukraine (http://www.nbuv.gov.ua/eb/ep.html) has the largest collection and gives access to the full texts of dissertation abstracts, scientific articles, classic works of Ukrainian literature, rare books, encyclopedias, dictionaries, and normative acts of Ukraine in the library and information sphere. The fullest list of links to other full-text collections is given here.

The electronic library of the National Parliamentary Library of Ukraine (http://profy.nplu.org/elibrary/index.htm) provides, among other materials, the full texts of laws and normative acts, as well as instructional materials on librarianship.

Regional libraries provide access primarily to their own collections and to materials on regional studies. They can be found through the sites of the Vernads'kyi National Library and the National Parliamentary Library.

The Library of the Verkhovna Rada (Supreme Council) of Ukraine (http://www.rada.kiev.ua/LIBRARY/text.htm) provides access to the texts of normative documents of foreign countries in Russian.

The V. Sukhomlyns'kyi State Pedagogical Research Library (http://www.library.edu-ua.net/) provides access to the works of Sukhomlyns'kyi.

In addition, the libraries of higher educational institutions have large electronic collections, but all of them provide access mostly onsite. Among them the largest collections belong to: Khmelnits'kyi National University (http://library.tup.km.ua/, approximately 1,000 university publications and 30,000 works of art), V. Karazin Kharkiv National University (http://www-ukr.univer.kharkov.ua/departments/library.php), Kyiv-Mohyla Academy National University of (http://www.library.ukma.kiev.ua/), and others.

In conclusion, it should be emphasized that, regrettably, there are no large-scale digitization projects underway at present in Ukraine, and this activity is not coordinated among libraries of different levels.

ELECTRONIC RESOURCES CREATED BY INSTITUTIONS OTHER THAN LIBRARIES

There are a considerable number of full-text resources created and presented on the Internet by entities other than libraries. Links to these materials are provided on many library websites, but none of them has a complete list. In addition, it is difficult to ensure that these lists reflect constantly changing information, as well as newly released material that is little publicized. The following are examples of sites referring to full-text resources in Ukraine:

- http://www.nbuv.gov.ua/portal/books.html#2–Page from website of V. Vernads'kyi National Library of Ukraine providing many links to Internet resources
- http://www.kniga.com.ua/–includes search system for e-books
- http://www.ukrlib.km.ru/ or http://ukrlib.com.ua/ - *Biblioteka ukrains' koi literatury* (Library of Ukrainian Literature)
- http://www.vesna.org.ua/–Server *Virtual'na Rus'*, containing *Vesna* library of Ukrainian literature
- http://ukrlife.org/main/library.html/–*Ukrains'ke zhyttia v Sevastopoli* (Ukrainian Life in Sevastopol) from Mariia Fisher-Slyzh Library
- http://www.proza.com.ua/–*Proza* site and its electronic library of prose works, http://www.lib.proza.com.ua/
- http://www.poezia.org/–*Poezia.org: poeziia ta avtors'ka pisnia Ukrainy* (Poetry and Author's Song of Ukraine)
- http://poetry.uazone.net/–*Poetyka: biblioteka ukrains'koi poezii* (Poetyka: Library of Ukrainian Poetry)
- http://www.pysar.net/–*Biblioteka koshovoho pysaria* (Library of the Koshovyi Writer), poetry
- http://www.fantasy.kiev.ua–works of fantasy (fiction)

VIRTUAL REFERENCE SERVICES PROVIDED BY UKRAINIAN LIBRARIES

During the last two years, more and more Ukrainian libraries have been implementing virtual reference services. These ventures are both cooperative projects by library associations and consortia, and efforts of individual libraries. For example, the National Ukrainian Library for Children has implemented a cooperative service called *Virtual'na bibliohrafychna dovidka: ob'iednana dovidkova sluzhba bibliotek Ukrainy* (Virtual Bibliographic Query: Ukrainian Libraries' Cooperative Reference Service, http://www.chl.kiev.ua/cgi-bin/sp/index.php); seven libraries participate. Reference queries are accepted in Russian and Ukrainian from all categories of users with no age restrictions. There is also an archive of queries (over 7,500) that can be searched or browsed. The State Library of Ukraine for Youth provides a virtual reference service for youth at http://www.4uth.gov.ua/6.htm, as does Luhans'k Oblast Youth Library, at http://lyl.lg.ua/virt_dovidka.php. Some regional libraries also provide virtual references service:

- Rivno–http://libr.rv.ua/
- Volyn–http://libr.fk.lutsk.ua/
- Luhans'k–http://www.library.lg.ua/
- Kherson–http://www.lib.kherson.ua/
- Dnipropetrovs'k–http://www.libr.dp.ua/
- Mykolaiev–http://www.niklib.com/

The National Parliamentary Library of Ukraine and the Library Information Portal provide virtual reference service on questions related to library activities (http://profy.nplu.org/ and http://www.librportal.org.ua, respectively).

Two Ukrainian libraries–M. L. Kropivnyts'kyi Mykolaiev Central Library (http://www.niklib.com) and the M. Gor'kii Kramatorsk Central City Library (http://www.lib-krm.org) in the Donetsk region–participate in an international virtual reference service for public libraries called *Virtual'naia spravka* (Virtual Information, http://www.library.ru/help/). This service is the cooperative effort of 20 libraries in Russia and 36 in other countries of the former Soviet Union. There is an archive of the queries already answered–24,000 total, from 300 Russian cities and 50 countries of the world.

NEW PROFESSIONAL JOURNAL FOR UKRAINIAN LIBRARIANS

Finally, a new professional journal for Ukrainian librarians began in 2003. Called *Bibliotechnyi forum Ukrainy* (Library Forum of Ukraine), it covers all aspects of library activities. It is edited by the present author and appears in paper and electronic formats, financed by the subscription agency Idea. The electronic version can be found on Idea's website, http://www.idea.com.ua/. Readers of *Slavic & East European Information Resources* are cordially invited to submit material to this journal.

doi:10.1300/J167v08n02_06

DIGITIZATION

The Methodological Advantages of Digital Editions: The Case of Eighteenth-Century Russian Texts

Marcus C. Levitt

SUMMARY. The post-Soviet period has seen major disagreements about how to edit Russian literary texts. This article first outlines some of the basic textological problems, starting with opposing definitions of *text* in either its critical (edited, optimized) or documentary (maximally authentic) hypostases. The article then examines problems involved in editing eighteenth-century Russian texts, offering examples from the

---

Marcus C. Levitt, PhD, is Associate Professor and Chair, Department of Slavic Languages and Literatures, University of Southern California, University Park, Los Angeles, CA 90089-4353 (E-mail: levitt@usc.edu).

[Haworth co-indexing entry note]: "The Methodological Advantages of Digital Editions: The Case of Eighteenth-Century Russian Texts." Levitt, Marcus C. Co-published simultaneously in *Slavic & East European Information Resources* (The Haworth Information Press, an imprint of The Haworth Press, Inc.) Vol. 8, No. 2/3, 2007, pp. 71-83; and: *Access to East European and Eurasian Culture: Publishing, Acquisitions, Digitization, Metadata* (ed: Miranda Remnek) The Haworth Information Press, an imprint of The Haworth Press, Inc., 2007, pp. 71-83. Single or multiple copies of this article are available for a fee from The Haworth Document Delivery Service [1-800-HAWORTH, 9:00 a.m. - 5:00 p.m. (EST). E-mail address: docdelivery@haworthpress.com].

Available online at http://seeir.haworthpress.com
© 2007 by The Haworth Press, Inc. All rights reserved.
doi:10.1300/J167v08n02_07

works of Alexander Sumarokov (1717-1777). The last section suggests ways in which digital editions may offer practical solutions to these problems and also greatly expand the value and accessibility of textual data, allowing for its multiple structuring and retrieval to meet the needs of the particular user. doi:10.1300/J167v08n02_07 *[Article copies available for a fee from The Haworth Document Delivery Service: 1-800-HAWORTH. E-mail address: <docdelivery@haworthpress.com> Website: <http://www. HaworthPress.com> © 2007 by The Haworth Press, Inc. All rights reserved.]*

KEYWORDS. Textology, editing, digital edition, digital archive, critical edition, orthography, eighteenth-century, Russian texts

TEXTOLOGY FROM A POST-SOVIET PERSPECTIVE

The period since the end of the Soviet Union may be seen as a time of crisis in text editing, of heterogeneity bordering on chaos–or, alternatively, as a time of creativity and experimentation. The grandiose edifice of Soviet text editing (one of its greatest philological achievements) has more or less collapsed into the commercial and intellectual turmoil of the free market, and most of its basic suppositions have been questioned, ignored, or rejected, and new solutions sought. Probably the most famous example of the current malaise of Russian textology is the ongoing edition of the complete academic works of Pushkin.[1] Virtually all practices of modern text editing have come into question–from the issue of what constitutes the primary text; the relative hierarchies of manuscript and print versions; how to order texts in an edition (e.g., by genre, by chronology, or by other orderings); to the problem of deciding which principles should govern the presentation of text, including the degree to which orthography and punctuation should be preserved or modernized. (Must we return to the pre-revolutionary orthography to fully appreciate the works of Dostoevskii or Boratynskii, for example?). The wide spectrum of response to these issues spans what some call hyper-scholarly, "postmodern" editions[2] to a variety of more or less popular critical editions, to commercially-oriented versions without any evident standards, and to reprinting pre-revolutionary publications and pirated knock-offs.

The same period has also witnessed the development of the web, whose existence has opened up the thinking and practice of text editing to the broader scholarly world. This leads to the basic argument of this article, that digital technology offers potential resolution of basic methodological problems involved in textology, and a quantum leap in making digital critical editions more effective information-managing tools. As a generality, this point may seem banal or self-evident, although it is just as clear that we have yet to fully utilize or comprehend much of the potential digital technologies afford; furthermore, in the practice of textology, the devil is in the details, as what may seem obvious theoretical truths or principles become seemingly intractable conundrums when we attempt to apply them in concrete situations.

Traditionally, perhaps the fundamental dilemma for text editors is to reconcile two competing notions of the text, its *critical* and *documentary* hypostases. Symptomatically, in the *Oxford English Dictionary* we find both ideas listed among competing definitions of the word *text*. On the one hand, text is:

> The wording adopted by an editor as (in his opinion) most nearly representing the author's original work; a book or edition containing this; also, with qualification, any form in which a writing exists or is current, as a *good, bad, corrupt, critical, received text*.

On the other, text means:

> The very words and sentences as originally written: a. in the original language, as opposed to a translation or rendering; b. in the original form and order, as distinguished from a commentary, marginal or other, or from annotations.[3]

The editor of a critical edition–the first kind of text–gathers and correlates all existent versions or witnesses of a work, locates and eliminates errors, and comes up with the "nearest representation" of the original work, the best or most genuine text; this commonly involves some degree of modernization (e.g., eliminating archaic letters), that is, modification, or *editing*. Probably the majority of scholars today have rejected the notion of a single, ideal or "original" text, but the idea of a critical text remains–a text as edited and aimed at a particular audience and with discrete goals. The notions of authenticity and authoritativeness have been challenged on practical and theoretical grounds, and critical editions in general are subject to the criticism that in reducing the multiplicity of possibilities down to one single canonical choice, an element of subjectivity on the part of the editor is inevitably present. (From one point of view, making explicit this inevitable limitation–the editor's subjectivity–constitutes the ultimate rationale and goal of critical editing, and the self-consciousness of this process is what marks its scientific, scholarly character). But the text here represents "the text as understood by a particular editor" and is only authoritative in these terms, despite appearances to the contrary.[4] (One example is Iakov Grot's monumental academy edition of Derzhavin of 1864-1883, which modernized his texts according to nineteenth-century norms that have since become outdated. Unfortunately, this remains the only full critical edition of his works.)

On the other hand, the documentary edition aims to reproduce the original materials as faithfully as possible, whether as a facsimile or in so-called "diplomatic," literal reproduction. Such an edition maximally preserves the original features of the work, possibly even down to errors and misprints, but also salvages those aspects of the text (e.g., graphic or linguistic peculiarities) that an editor might not appreciate or recognize and that might be lost in a "critically edited" version.[5] Like the critical edition, documentary editions envision a particular audience (usually specialists), and have their own practical, cultural, and theoretical associations, which may also be problematic and limiting in various ways. In relation to eighteenth-century texts, for example, it has been argued that a "diplomatic" approach associates these texts with medievalist textological practices, assigning them antiquarian or archaeological rather than living aesthetic value. Aspects of the text that might have been neutral (not carriers of meaning) to an eighteenth-century audience may carry misleading associations for twenty-first century readers. Another example of a pitfall of the documentary as opposed to a critical approach is the 1935 facsimile ("photo-lithographic") edition of Radishchev's *Journey from St. Petersburg to Moscow*,[6] which reproduced what turned out to be an anomalous version of the work, whose printed texts were far from uniform. The very "scientific" superiority of the documentary approach defines its limitations.

In sum, then, is the job of the text editor basically archaeological, defining the text in all of its historical specificity, placing "absolute trust in the text with all of its [presumed] constituent elements,"[7] or editorial and aesthetic, restoring wholeness and consistency to works of art and making them accessible to a modern audience?

THE EIGHTEENTH CENTURY HORNET'S NEST

The problem I have outlined here is especially thorny and intractable as regards eighteenth- and early nineteenth-century Russian texts, insofar as the norms of that age were in active flux, and it is often nearly or actually impossible to determine what the *Oxford English Dictionary* definition refers to as the "author's original work," that is, the degree of authorial intent reflected in a given instantiation of his or her work. I will take the problem of capitalization in Alexander Sumarokov's texts as just one example, which will also serve as an introduction to some of the specific problems of dealing with his corpus.

A few words of background. Sumarokov (1717-77), who was one of the major writers of his day, bemoaned the lack of institutions that could have established and regulated orthographic norms–a language assembly, schools, the lack of an authoritative dictionary and grammar textbook–and while he clearly had the idea of holding up his own works as a model, he was painfully aware of the Sisyphean obstacle of proliferating inferior usage that seemed to grow geometrically worse over time.[8] As an Academy of Sciences translator complained two years after Sumarokov's death, "great disagreements, uncertainties and difficulties [make] the spelling of almost every writer or translator in some way different from the rest."[9] At the same time, there was ample debate and disagreement about what the norms should be, so that despite the seeming chaos, the situation could endow the use of particular forms with great semiotic potential, marking them as "meaning-bearing" elements. Indeed entire treatises could be written about the preference for particular grammatical forms. As V. M. Zhivov has brilliantly shown in his *Iazyk i kul'tura v Rossii XVIII veka* (Language and Culture in Russia of the Eighteenth Century) (Moscow: Iazyki russkoi kul'tury, 1996), the development of the new literary language, from alphabet to grammar to spelling, was intimately tied up with fundamental issues of cultural self-definition, which were thrashed out in debates over the norms of a vernacular literature. This was especially the case with orthographic norms, as the Petrine reform of the literary tongue–or, more properly, the demand that such a tongue be created–was graphically marked by a newly-devised alphabet.

Furthermore, while Sumarokov was deeply involved in these debates, and his views were known and clearly had a certain influence, determining their precise extent–both his theoretical ideas about orthography, laid out in various published and unpublished writings, and their actual, practical implementation–presents a whole series of interpretive difficulties.[10] To take but one example, in Sumarokov's essay "O pravopisanii"(On Spelling), he criticized the use of excessive capital letters, which he took to be a French, and especially German, practice.[11] He argued that capitals should only be used at the start of a sentence or a line of verse, and suggested that this even apply to the word "god," i.e., that it as well as pronouns and adjectives relating to the deity should be capitalized only at the start of a sentence or line of verse. Significant here is not only Sumarokov's opinion, but also the fact that the form in which his essay was printed–in Nikolai Novikov's posthumous full works of 1781-82 (2nd ed.,1787)–does not reflect the very orthographic rule it lays out (i.e., it was full of "excessive" capital letters). What are we to make of this?

Sumarokov's archive did not survive Novikov's arrest and exile, and this publication is our only source for this work. In republishing this essay, should we "recreate" an unattested "authorial text," changing capitals to small letters? Yet Sumarokov's other published works do not follow this rule, and other instances of his orthographic recommendations likewise remained purely theoretical, on paper. How meaningful should we consider capitalization to be as a carrier of cultural or aesthetic value? In contrast, for the eighth volume of Lomonosov's complete works (1953-80), the editors, while modernizing the orthography, preserved the capitalization "in order to reproduce more precisely the system of external ornamentation of his poetic and rhetorical texts."[12] To what extent is capitalization–or the use of any letters of the pre-revolutionary alphabet, for that matter–a component of the visual and aesthetic meaning conveyed by the "external" (visual) aspect of a text? [13] In an article related to the then forthcoming edition of Karamzin's *Pis'ma russkogo puteshestvennika* (Letters of a Russian Traveler, published in 1987), which preserved the use of capitals, Iu. M. Lotman, N. I. Tolstoi, and B. A. Uspenskii argued for their significance. They referred back to the discrepancy between Sumarokov's statement and Novikov's editorial practices, and argued that, for Novikov, capitalization on the German model was a purposeful literary practice, with which they associated that of Karamzin.[14]

V. A. Zapadov in turn challenged this argument for a "Novikovian" German-modeled system of capitalization in his edition of Radishchev's *Puteshestvie iz Peterburga v Moskvu* five years later (1992), which did not preserve eighteenth-century (inconsistent) capitalization of non-proper nouns and adjectives. Zapadov argued that such capitalization might well not have represented Novikov's design, but that of particular typesetters and proofreaders at the Moscow University typography where he printed his publications. Indeed, Sumarokov's writings also offer ample material concerning the problematic role of various intermediaries–the copyist (*kopiist* or *perepischik*), the censor (*tsenzor*), typesetter (*naborshchik*), proofreader (*korrektor*), editor-proofreader (*spravshchik*), and editor-publisher (*redaktor* or *izdatel'*)–in the process of transforming the authorial manuscript into final published text. Perhaps his most famous manifesto on language was addressed "K tipografskim naborshchikam" (To Typesetters) (1759), offering his ideas on language in the form of advice as to how his works should be typeset and criticizing many current practices. Concerning capitalization, in "O pravopisanii" Sumarokov specifically complains that ". . . I begin by using lower case letters, but in my absence typesetters, thinking that I made a mistake in my manuscript, put capitals in their place."[15] He also complains about ignorant writers "who give authority over their works to them, not knowing themselves how to cope with spelling."[16] Elsewhere he explains typesetters' over-eagerness for capitals as a concern with *lèse majesté,* in emulation of petty bureaucrats who are given to excessively servile capitalization to avoid charges of lack of respect. What then are we to do–reproduce a chaotic variability, or bite the bullet and make the editorial decision to regularize usage on the basis of a norm we will define, while understanding that the seemingly chaotic variability might conceal other patterns of order and information?

This is but one example. The special case of capitalizing "god" and referent adjectives and pronouns has its own specific problems, both due to heterogeneous practices in the eighteenth century, and because of ideologically-motivated lower-casing in the Soviet period, which has sometimes given way in turn to equally automatic upper-casing.

How can one resolve this problem, if it is resolvable? First of all, we should repeat that the theoretical postulate (e.g., what "most nearly represents the author's original work"–what Russians refer to as *avtorskaia volia* [authorial will])–is not of much help, and what is needed is not only extensive and painstaking investigation of the primary documents but also a well-thought-out research strategy, involving linguistic and statistical analysis. To start, this includes a thorough examination of the existing manuscripts in Sumarokov's hand, those corrected by him, or those he wrote as corrected by others (e.g., by journal editors); as well as a correlation with the published witnesses (variants) and any other relevant material. In turn, these need to be juxtaposed to Sumarokov's stated positions on language (as in "O pravopisanii"), both for clues about significant usage, and also so that theory may be compared to practice. (As in traditional text editing, an intimate knowledge of the material is indispensable, and will in large part determine the textological strategies.)

Understanding the Sumarokov corpus, however, is only one aspect of the issue. It is impossible to define Sumarokov's authorial practice in isolation, without setting it within the broader context of contemporary practice–those of the particular typesetter, typography, journal, and authorial cohort. This, of course, is an incomparably more labor-intensive and complex task, as it involves the identification of the corpus of material to be examined and defining of the analytical tools or categories to be explored. At the present moment, and using pen and paper tools (e.g., the trusty Soviet-era *kartoteka* [card file]!), this would appear to be the work of several lifetimes. The potential corpus of material is huge (all of eighteenth-century civic print production),[17] so that preliminary research would need to be done to identify specific discrete bodies of material to be targeted for analysis. Research is required to formulate hypotheses, and appropriate analytical tools and methods would need to be developed to test them. On the one hand, after a certain statistically-defined point, this material would supply a basis on which to make comparisons and judge variation; on the other, over time it would be able to identify and clarify patterns of usage and traditions or trends within the larger, more heterogeneous body of material. The possible existence of a "Novikov" system of capitalization, for example, might emerge from such comparative analysis, and offer a starting point for inquiry.[18] Such a statistical analysis would, at least, provide a quantification of the "chaos" reigning in eighteenth-century textual practices.

DIGITAL SOLUTIONS

So far, I have talked about issues that seem to deal only with issues of print and books, but it could be argued that the division of the dual aspects of this year's Fisher Forum into Print Culture and Digital Applications–while designed to cater to a broad range of interests–is somewhat artificial, since the future developments in print (or book) culture may well be found, in part, in the application of digital technologies to book production. In other words, digital applications represent an extension and enrichment of print culture, and of textological strategies, and not their antithesis. We may also put this in terms of *text,* going beyond the "critical" and "documentary" dichotomy described above, toward a notion not of materiality (texts on vellum, printed on paper, or digitalized and displayed on a computer screen), or a product delimited by front and back covers, but of process. The etymological root for text, as MacKenzie reminds us, is from the word for *weaving.*[19] We move from an abstract model of computing whose basic metaphor is one of the brain (artificial intelligence) to that of the book–the computer as an incredibly powerful prosthetic book that expands the fundamental things that books can do (cross referencing, indexing, etc.) and adding hyper-textual and hypermedia features that give a quantum increase in a book's analytical potential.[20] The potential is in the direction of the presentation of material and the new analytical methods that are possible–both areas under active experiment and development.

From what I have said so far, two kinds of projects emerge, a digital edition of Sumarokov, which would account for multiple variants of his works; and a large-corpora database of eighteenth-century texts that could be used to do a statistical analysis of linguistic norms. On some level, these two projects are analogs, and part of a larger notion of knowledge in process, organized as text.

Some scholars purposely avoid the word *edition* as connected to traditional editing practices and the creation of a finite product, and prefer instead *archive* or even *library*, both of which suggest an open-ended repository and resource that can be utilized in a multiplicity of ways both in terms of content and interactivity. Another synonym or analogue might be the website–a locus for the intersection of multiple texts, a web that is connected to a potentially infinite number of other webs, and whose usage depends on the specific needs of the user. The digital edition allows the text to be woven, unwoven into its component parts, and rewoven into new combinations–among other things, dramatically exposing the fallacy (or simply, the insufficiency) of the single, authoritative, canonical text. This is one of its principle advantages over the printed, book edition, which more or less demands a focus on a single, central "best text." A digital edition can seamlessly combine the critical and documentary aspects of the text, allowing readers to navigate their way through the choices. Again, a main point is that hypertext obviates the demand to make a single choice of one text among many (although such a choice may be offered and made), but by the nature of electronic interface, dramatizes in a direct and immediate way the multiplicity of elements that comprise the "text."[21]

One of these elements that I have hardly touched on so far is their hypermedia potential. I could envisage, for example, an edition of Sumarokov's verse *nadpisi* (poetic inscriptions) that would interface with images of the monuments described. I could imagine his songs published in parallel with musical scores (e.g., those in G. N. Teplov's 1759 songbook *Mezhdu delom bezdel'e ili Sobranie raznykh pesen . . .* Between Action Inaction, or, Collection of Various Songs . . ., *in* which the songs were published without permission,[22] or to manuscript collections),[23] and his operas and ballet linked not only to visual materials (e.g., sketches for the set designs by Antonio Peresinotti and Giuseppe Valeriani) but also to audiovisual recordings of performances (e.g., the recent staging at the Marinsky theater of Francesco Araia's opera *Tsefal [Cephalus] and Procris*, for which Sumarokov wrote the libretto).[24] Sumarokov's *basni* (fables) that were pirated for anonymous *liubki* could be paired with their commercial interpretations.[25] Of course the challenge here, as with other digital applications, is not merely the choice of what to present, but how to do it, how to conceptualize the multi-media nature of texts ("texts" also in a broader sense as the weaving together of various media) and develop the appropriate tools to deal with them. Like an archive or library, the digital edition is thus at any given moment complete yet open to further development. Like an archive or library, it has no necessary preconceived starting point, and the flexibility of its hypertextual tools and its interfaces determine its multiplicity of uses.

If the digital edition focused on a *single* author comprises a cultural text on the micro level, a database of *collected* texts–for which a collection like *FEB* (Fundamental'naia elektronnia biblioteka literatury i fol'klory [Fundamental Digital Library of Russian Literature and Folklore]) might offer a prototype source pool[26]–could be mined for contextualizing the changing linguistic norms on the macro level. Yet, as we have noted, the basic nature of the digital edition, as opposed to that in print, is the relativization or decentering of authority, allowing for multiple structuring of data. Hence the micro/macro distinction itself is contingent. If the immediate goal I have in mind is of a digitalized Sumarokov, it could easily become the point of departure for an entire web–a web of other webs.

NOTES

1. See, for example, the following exchange over its editorial principles: Verner Leifel'dt, "Modernizatsiia tekstov Pushkina i ee posledstviia" (Modernization of Pushkin's Texts and Its Consequences), *Novoe literaturnoe obozrenie* 33 (1998): 161-184; and V. E. Vatsuro, "Eshche raz ob akademicheskom izdanii Pushkina: razbor kriticheskikh zamechanii prof. Vernera Leifel'dta" (Once More Concerning the Academic Edition of Pushkin: Selection of the Critical Comments of Prof. Verner Leifel'dt), *Novoe literaturnoe obozrenie* 37 (1999): 253-267. See also the discussion in Iu. M. Lotman, "K probleme novogo akademicheskogo izdaniia Pushkina," *Pushkin* (St. Petersburg: Iskusstvo-SPB, 1995), 369-73.

2. See Jerome McGann, *Radiant Textuality: Literature After the World Wide Web* (New York: Palgrave, 2001), chap. 3.

3. OED [*Oxford English Dictionary*] Online, "text n.[1]," http://dictionary.oed.com/cgi/entry/50250103?query_type=word&queryword=text&first=1&max_to_show=10&sort_type=alpha&result_place=1&search_id=Lktz-UhADiO-4943&hilite=50250103 (accessed July 31, 2006).

4. As the editors of the series *Literaturnye pamiatniki* (Literary Monuments) put it, "A publication with maximal preservation of the orthographic peculiarities of a particular edition . . . inevitably presumes some measure of reconstruction carried out by the publisher-editor (*publikatorom*). The result of this reconstruction is not an objective literary reality–'the text of a given work by a given writer'–but, necessarily, 'the text of a given writer in light of the conception of a given publisher'." Quoted by V. A. Zapadov in A. N. Radishchev, *Puteshestvie iz Peterburga v Moskvu; Vol'nost'* (Journey from St. Petersburg to Moscow; Freedom), ed. V. A. Zapadov (St. Petersburg: Nauka, 1992), 632.

5. On the one hand, there are those who argue that only those "meaning-bearing" elements need to be preserved, as opposed to those that are "neutral," meaning often defined in terms of the "author's will" (elements that the author consciously chose; thus "meaning-bearing" elements may usually be identified when there is a choice between two or more variant forms). See, for example, Iu. M. Lotman, N. I. Tolstoi, and B. A. Uspenskii, "Nekotorye voprosy tekstologii i publikatsii russkikh literaturnykh pamiatnikov XVIII veka" (Some Questions on the Textology and Publication of Russian Literary Monuments of the Eighteenth Century), *Izvestiia Akademii nauk SSSR, Seriia literatury i iazyka* 40, no. 4 (1981): 312-24. On the other hand, as D. F. McKenzie has argued, every aspect of a text, material and scribal, bears meaning: "In pursuit of historical meanings, we move from the most minute feature of the material form of the book to questions of authorial, literary and social context. These all bear in turn on the ways in which texts are then re-read, re-edited, re-designed, re-printed, and republished." *Bibliography and the Sociology of Texts* (New York: Cambridge University Press, 1999), 14. A critical editor, by contrast, makes a decision based on her or his level of understanding of the text, as well as that of the target audience; all else is ignored, lost or distorted.

6. A. N. Radishchev, *Puteshestvie iz Peterburga v Moskvu*, 2 vols. (Moscow: Academia, 1935).

7. T. V. Artem'eva, introduction, *Mysli o dushe: Russkaia metafizika XVIII veka* (Thoughts about the Soul: Russian Metaphysics of the Eighteenth Century), ed. T. V. Artem'eva (St. Petersburg: Nauka, 1996), 69.

8. See my discussion in: "The Barbarians Among Us, or Sumarokov's Views on Orthography," in *Eighteenth-Century Russia: Society, Culture, Economy, Papers from the VII International Conference of the Study Group on Eighteenth-Century Russia, Wittenberg 2004*, ed. Roger Bartlett and Gabriela Lehmann-Carli (Münster: LIT-Verlag, 2007), forthcoming. For an introduction to Sumarokov's life and works, see my "Aleksandr Petrovich Sumarokov," in *Early Modern Russian Writers, Late Seventeenth and Eighteenth Centuries*, ed. Marcus C. Levitt, *Dictionary of Literary Biography*, vol. 150 (Detroit, New York, London: Bruccoli Clark Layman, and Gale Research, 1995), 370-381; available online at http://galenet.galegroup.com/servlet/LitRC?vrsn=

3&OP=contains&locID=usc13562&srchtp=athr&ca=1&c=1&ste=6&tab=1&tbst=arp& ai=U13724078&n=10&docNum=H1200004747&ST=sumarokov&bConts=8879 (subscription necessary; accessed July 31, 2006).

9. V. P. Svetov, *Opyt novogo rossiiskogo pravopisaniia* (Attempt at a New Russian Orthography) (St. Petersburg: Akademiia nauk, 1773), 7.

10. Levitt, "The Barbarians," passim.

11. A. P. Sumarokov, *Polnoe sobranie vsekh sochinenii, v stikhakh i proze* (Complete Collection of All Works in Verse and Prose), ed. N. I. Novikov (Moscow: Novikov, 1787), 10:5-38. Henceforth referred to as *PSVS*.

12. M. V. Lomonosov, *Polnoe sobranie sochinenii* (Complete Collected Works) (Moscow: Akademia nauk 1959), 8:862.

13. Do we postulate a "Baroque," ornamental (visual) aspect here, to be contrasted to a "Neo-classicist" desire for greater linguistic (and orthographic) transparency? Without proof, this is but one of many subjective decisions a critical editor may perform. This editorial decision may also take into consideration issues connected with particular genres (e.g., particular spelling or grammatical practices associated with odes).

14. Lotman, Tolstoi, and Uspenskii, "Nekotorye voprosy," 317.

15. Sumarokov, *PSVS*, 10:36.

16. Sumarokov, *PSVS*, 10:32.

17. See the *Svodnyi katalog russkoi knigi grazhdanskoi pechati XVIII veka, 1725-1800* (Union Catalog of the Civic Print Russian Book of the Eighteenth Century, 1725-1800), 5 vols. (Moscow: Kniga, 1962-1975).

18. My own sense is that there will not turn out to be a "Novikov" system, but various practices in competition concerning what nouns should be capitalized–a combination of the practices of specific typographies, typographers, and editors. In contrast, a "German" system implies that every noun be capitalized.

19. McKenzie, *Bibliography*, 5-6.

20. My argument here is greatly indebted to Jerome McGann. See his *Radiant Textology*, especially chap. 2 ("The Rationale of Hypertext"), available online at http://www.iath.virginia.edu/public/jjm2f/rationale.html (accessed July 31, 2006); and his (with Dino Buzetti) "Critical Editing in a Digital Horizon," in *Electronic Textual Editing*, ed. Lou Burnard, Katherine O'Brien O'Keeffe, and John Unsworth (New York: Modern Language Association of America, 2006), 94-127, online at http://www.tei-c.org/Activities/ETE/Preview/mcgann.xml (accessed July 31, 2006).

21. Among the pioneering English-language projects, see: Jerome McGann's *Rosetti Archive* (http://www.rossettiarchive.org/); the *William Blake Archive* (http://www.blakearchive.org/blake/); Kevin Kiernan's edition of *Beowulf* (http://www.uky.edu/~kiernan/eBeowulf/guide.htm), which was published in CD-ROM (*Electronic Beowulf*, ed. Kevin Kiernan with Andrew Prescott et al., 2 disks [London: British Library; Ann Arbor, MI: University of Michigan Press, 1999]); and Peter Robinson's *The Electronic Canterbury Tales* (http://afdtk.uaa.alaska.edu/ect_main.htm), on which see his "Electronic Textual Editing: The Canterbury Tales and other Medieval Texts," online at http://www.tei-c.org/Activities/ETE/Preview/robinson.xml?style=text; this article cites several other current projects. (All of these sites were accessed July 31, 2006.)

22. Teplov's texts are republished in T. N. Livanova, *Russkaia muzykal'naia kul'tura XVIII veka v ee sviaziakh s literaturoi, teatrom i bytom: issledovaniia i materialy* (Russian Musical Culture of the Eighteenth Century in Its Relations with Literature, Theater, and Life: Studies and Materials) (Moscow: Gos. Muzykal'noe izdatel' stvo, 1952), 1:189-245; see Livanova's discussion on pp. 66-67.

23. See, for example, the song attributed to Sumarokov in the recently published collection *Rukopisnyi pesennik XVIII veka* (Manuscript Songbook of the Eighteenth Century) in the series *Muzykal'nyi Peterburg, Entsiklopedicheskii slovar', XVIII vek,* (Musical St. Petersburg: Encyclopedic Dictionary, Eighteenth Century), vol. 1, bk. 5 (St. Petersburg: Kompozitor, 2002), 30-31; on the attribution see pp. 184-185. These manuscript songbooks still largely await study.

24. Theatrical program for Francesco Araia, *Tsefal and Procris*, and Domenico Cimarosa, *La Cleopatra*, St. Petersburg: Marinsky Theater, June 14, 2001. See also Marcus C. Levitt, "Sumarokov's *Sanctuary of Virtue* (1759) as 'the First Russian Ballet,' *Experiment/Eksperiment* 10 (2004): 51-84.

25. A. V. Kokorev, "Sumarokov i russkie narodnye kartinki" (Sumarokov and Russian Folk Paintings), *Uchenye zapiski Moskovskogo gos. universiteta* 127, *Trudy Kafedry russkoi literatury* (1948): 227-236. *Liubki* (plural of *liubok*) are "popular literature, either a graphic with text or, in later years, a short work of fiction printed on cheap paper for a lower-class audience," according to James von Geldern and Louise McReynolds, *Entertaining Tsarist Russia: Tales, Songs, Plays, Movies, Jokes, Adds, and Images from Russian Urban Life, 1779 to 1917* (Bloomington: Indiana University Press, 1998), 391.–Ed. (KR)

26. Joseph Peschio, Igor Pil'shchikov, and Konstantin Vigurskii, "Academic Digital Libraries Russian Style: An Introduction to *The Fundamental Digital Library of Russian Literature and Folklore*," in *Virtual Slavica: Digital Libraries, Digital Archives*, ed. Michael Neubert, special issue, *Slavic & East European Information Resources* 6, no. 2-3 (2005): 45-64. Notably, this library has no eighteenth-century materials yet, although they are part of its planned expansion.

doi:10.1300/J167v08n02_07

Internet Resources on Russian History: The Electronic Library at Moscow State University

Leonid Borodkin
Timur Valetov

SUMMARY. The *Elektronnaia biblioteka* (Electronic Library) of the Faculty of History at Moscow State University (MGU) holds online texts that relate to different periods of global history. It contains about 100 texts on Russian history electronically published within the MGU project, as well as links to hundreds of other historical sources on Russian history on the Internet. Project texts are usually accompanied by short annotations with comments on the role of the document in Russian history. Another important component of the Electronic Library is an example of a topic-oriented historical Internet resource (TOHIR) on Russian/Soviet labor history. Online access to the catalog of resources within the TOHIR is provided on the basis of MySQL and PHP-scripts. doi:10.1300/J167v08n02_08 *[Article copies available for a fee from The Haworth Document Delivery Service:*

Leonid Borodkin is Professor and Head, Department for Historical Information Science, Moscow Lomonosov State University, Uchebnyi Korpus 1, Leninskie Gory, Moscow 119899, Russia (E-mail: borodkin@hist.msu.ru).

Timur Valetov is an assistant in the Historical Information Science Laboratory, Department for Historical Information Science, Moscow Lomonosov State University, Uchebnyi Korpus 1, Leninskie Gory, Moscow 119899, Russia (E-mail: tim@hist. msu.ru).

[Haworth co-indexing entry note]: "Internet Resources on Russian History: The Electronic Library at Moscow State University." Borodkin, Leonid, and Timur Valetov. Co-published simultaneously in *Slavic & East European Information Resources* (The Haworth Information Press, an imprint of The Haworth Press, Inc.) Vol. 8, No. 2/3, 2007, pp. 85-93; and: *Access to East European and Eurasian Culture: Publishing, Acquisitions, Digitization, Metadata* (ed: Miranda Remnek) The Haworth Information Press, an imprint of The Haworth Press, Inc., 2007, pp. 85-93. Single or multiple copies of this article are available for a fee from The Haworth Document Delivery Service [1-800-HAWORTH, 9:00 a.m. - 5:00 p.m. (EST). E-mail address: docdelivery@haworthpress.com].

Available online at http://seeir.haworthpress.com
© 2007 by The Haworth Press, Inc. All rights reserved.
doi:10.1300/J167v08n02_08

1-800-HAWORTH. E-mail address: <docdelivery@haworthpress.com> Website: <http://www.HaworthPress.com> © 2007 by The Haworth Press, Inc. All rights reserved.]

KEYWORDS. Moscow State University, Russia, historical texts, Russian history, primary sources, labor history, Electronic Library

THE ELECTRONIC LIBRARY AND ITS CONTENTS

The *Elektronnaia biblioteka* (Electronic Library) is an important part of the website of the Faculty of History at Moscow Lomonosov State University.[1] It aims to provide students and scholars with Internet access to the resources necessary for education and research in history. Special attention is paid to the task of making available online a substantial number of full electronic versions of historical documents.

These texts are related to different periods of global history, and they range from resources like the Babylonian code of laws (issued by Hammurabi, ruler of most of Mesopotamia in the eighteenth century BC) to the Soviet Constitution of 1977. However, there is a particular emphasis on primary sources for the study of Russian history of different periods. Almost all the texts in the Electronic Library are presented in Russian; this is why the English version of the library's table of contents (TOC) links directly to the sources originally written in Russian (or in Old Russian). Hence, the English version of that part of the library consists of only three main sections (instead of 12 sections as in the Russian version).[2] They are devoted first to Medieval Russian history (before the eighteenth century), secondly to the history of the Russian Empire and, finally, to twentieth-century Russian history.

This part of the Electronic Library (that is, the content of three of the 12 sections on the Russian table of contents) holds about 114 texts on Russian history electronically published within our project, and also provides links to hundreds of other historical sources on Russian history located elsewhere on the Internet. Our own publications are normally accompanied by short annotations with comments on the role of each document in Russian history. The quality of the texts presented on the other websites to which we link is different, but our strategy in bringing these links together is to allow researchers to find as many historical texts in Russian as possible. We carefully select authentic sources; so, for example, the electronic version of *Velesova kniga* (Book of Veles)–which was proved to be a forgery–is not presented in the list.[3] We do not include articles or research studies.

The basis of the Electronic Library consists of different legislative codes. It begins with *Russkaia Pravda* (Russian Justice), the oldest known Slavic legal code issued by Prince Jaroslav the Wise and his successors in the eleventh to twelfth centuries. We also provide links to the legal code of Pskov of the fifteenth century, and the *Sudebnik* (Code of Laws) of 1497 by Ivan III. The fundamental *Sobornoe ulozhenie* (Code of Laws) of 1649–which was an attempt to describe all kinds of criminal, civil and clerical offences and punishments–is also presented in our Electronic Library in its full version consisting of 25 chapters (about 350 pages). The epoch of reforms related to the reign of Peter the Great is presented with a set of basic legal acts; among them are those establishing the Senate (1711 and 1722), the first division of the country into eight provinces (1708), the well-known Table of Ranks describing the order of civil and military service of the nobility, the *Artikul voinskii* (Military Code) of 1715, the code of the civil service of 1720 (the General Regulation), and the custom service regulation of 1724.

We also present several very important legal acts that were ratified during the period of the Russian Empire such as the *Gramota na prava, vol'nosti i preimushchestva blagorodnogo rossiiskogo dvorianstva* (Charter to the Russian Nobility) issued by Catherine the Great in April 1785. (Not linked here, but available from the Russian section of the site, is the companion *Gramota na prava i vygody gorodam Rossiiskoi imperii* [Charter to the Towns]–also issued on the same date). Other acts provided here include those related to the emancipation of serfdom such as the Manifesto of February 19, 1861. In addition, the researcher will find the 1905 October Manifesto in which Tsar Nicholas II agreed to a form of universal suffrage for elections to the Parliament (Gosudarstvennaia Duma), and the *Vysochaishe utverzhdennye Osnovnye Gosudarstvennye Zakony* (Fundamental Laws) of 1906, prescribing the new principles of governing the Empire.

The Revolutionary period is presented by the text (and an actual image that can be enlarged for easy reading) of the act of abdication of March 1917 of the last Russian tsar, Nicholas II (*Ob otrechenii Gosudaria Imperatora Nikolaia II ot prestola Rossiiskogo i o slozhenii s sebia verkhovnoi vlasti*). Also included are the set of basic decrees of the Bolshevik government of 1917-1918 (*Deklaratsiia Vremennogo pravitel'stva o ego sostave i zadachakh*). All the Soviet Constitutions (of 1918, 1924, 1936 and 1977) are presented as well.

Next, the Electronic Library also contains a number of official texts, which played as important a role in Russian history as that played by legal acts. In the section entitled Russia from the Eighteenth to the Beginning of the Twentieth Century, researchers will find a set of Russian treaties with different foreign countries, from 1721 (the Treaty of Nystad, which ended the Great Northern War) to 1915, the Entente Treaty devoted to the status of the Straights of Constantinople (to be realized in the event of the Entente's victory in World War I). In the section entitled Russia Up to the Eighteenth Century there is a set of testaments (*dukhovnye gramoty*) of the princes of Muscovy from the fourteenth to the sixteenth centuries. This dynamic set is a very good source for tracing changes in the estates and policies of Russian princes (later, tsars) who gathered ancient Russian lands under the control of its new capital, Moscow.

Another text of great significance to be found in the same section is the sixteenth-century *Domostroi* (Household Management), the code of rules and advice for everyday life and family relations. This text is probably the best source for studying Orthodox clerical regulation of all facets of everyday life in medieval Russian society. Providing an astonishing range of detail, it prescribes how to go to church and how to help the indigent, how to teach children and how to heal diseases, how to organize holidays and how to grow vegetables. However, the most important material in this source is the set of rules prescribing medieval orthodox family relations, with the almost ultimate power of the head of the family over its other members.

Not only official acts but opposition treatises on how to rule the country are very interesting. The Russian revolutionary movement is represented in a set of proclamations and programs from a variety of revolutionaries and illegal political organizations. These include Nikolai Chernyshevsky's individual proclamation of 1861, *Barskim krest'ianam ot ikh dobrozhelatelei poklon* (To the Peasants of the Nobility). As noted on our website, this proclamation was the most famous work from a series of radical-democratic printed critiques on the methods of carrying out the emancipation; addressed to peasants, it attempted, in accessible language, to explain that the reform carried an extortionate character, and did *not* better the life of peasants. Also available for the following decade is the program of May 1878 put out by the revolutionary secret society known as Zemlia i Volia (Land and Liberty).

Memoirs and non-official writings are perhaps the most interesting documents of past epochs. Our Electronic Library contains a number of these materials, and also provides many links to such materials presented on other websites. One of the most remarkable publications (presented in our library) is *O Rossii v tsarstvovanie Alekseia Mikhailovicha* (On Russia Under the Reign of Tsar Alexis Mikhailovich) written by Grigory Kotoshikhin–a Foreign Office official who defected to Poland in 1664 and later to Sweden, and who wrote all he knew about the Russian government, army, foreign office, and everyday life in Moscow. Another very interesting text is *Pis'ma iz derevni* (Letters from the Countryside) from 1872-1887, written by Alexander Engelgardt. The author was a scientist, expelled from a university for his overly liberal opinions. He later lived on his country estate, conducted some more-or-less successful experiments in agricultural management and wrote these very multifaceted observations on the style of life of the Russian post-emancipation peasantry. The third such author presented in our Electronic Library is Alexander Spiridovich, former general of gendarmes and head of the Kiev gendarmerie in 1903-1905, who emigrated after 1917 and wrote his memoirs entitled *Zapiski zhandarma* (Notes of a Policeman) about the period from 1891 to 1905.

The list of historical source texts and links to such texts forms the core of the Electronic Library, but it holds some additional data. Among the data is a large collection of links to libraries, archives, and museums (art and history) around the world. There are links to more than 80 Russian museums and almost 550 museums abroad. The link collection is also available in English.

Another part of the library is called Digital Sources. Images of historical documents and other materials are to be presented here. Now it contains images of archival records of *Massaria Caffae*, an account book of the Caffa (Genoese colony in Crimea) Treasury for the year of 1374, and a collection of portraits of Patriarch Nikon. A handbook on Russian eighteenth-century watermarks is in our immediate plans for electronic publication.

The Electronic Library is one of the most popular sections of the Faculty of History website. Its main page alone receives 12,000 to 15,000 visits per month, and many of its pages are at the very top of the list of visits to the website. The Electronic Library is also one of the most often cited parts of the website, and this is not surprising, because it is the part of the website that is specially planned to be interesting to a wide range of researchers, students, and those who are interested in history.

TOPIC-ORIENTED HISTORICAL INTERNET RESOURCE SITES

In addition to its provision of a range of historical source material online, the Electronic Library of the History Faculty of Moscow State University contains an important component which illustrates our approach to the building of topic-oriented historical Internet resource (TOHIR) sites. We have in mind the TOHIR entitled *Labor History: From Russia's Pre-Revolutionary Industrialization to Soviet Industrialization, 1880s-1930s* (http://www.hist.msu.ru/Labor/index.html).

This resource presents all important aspects of Russia's labor history of the period mentioned above including labor relations, institutional history, labor conflicts, sociocultural aspects, workers' everyday life, and anthropological issues. In the process of forming this TOHIR we were guided by our desire to create a comprehensive collection of digitized materials that would represent the variety of related historical sources, historiography, bibliography, databases, and references to other related Internet resources.

Most of the materials presented in our TOHIR are digitized copies of "paper" originals. We give the complete bibliographical (or archival) references in all such cases. We used different formats to digitize paper materials. Many are presented in both .pdf and .doc formats to satisfy users' facilities. In all cases the user can see the total number of pages as indicated in the corresponding (original) publication.

To provide efficient access and search facilities at our website, we installed a search engine and ftp-access to the collection of files. Recently we finalized work on the creation of a problem-oriented thesaurus which includes more than 200 lexical elements distributed at seven hierarchical levels. The semantic network contains about 250 links among the lexical elements. Each descriptor is provided with an article that includes information on synonyms and associated elements, as well as on related elements located at other hierarchical levels. Online access to the catalog of resources is provided on the basis of MySQL and PHP-scripts.[4]

The structure of our TOHIR is based on our classification of the materials presented. It currently includes 12 types (collections) of digitized materials listed in the main menu. Here we give a brief description of our TOHIR contents:

The first collection contains the most important documents issued by the state to regulate labor relations in Russian industries in both pre-Revolutionary and Soviet times. Amounting to almost 30 documents covering the period from the 1880s to the 1930s, the collection includes, for example, the directive of June 1 1882, *O maloletnykh rabotaiushchikh na zavodakh, fabrikakh i manufakturakh* (On Children Working in Factories, Mills, and Manufacturing Establishments).

The second collection presents some of the principal directories on industrial labor in Russia and the USSR, and statistical publications of the Factory Inspectorate, materials from the First All-Russia's Population Census (1897), chronicles of workers' movements, and similar materials. Among the texts represented here are accounts of factory inspectors from the period 1900-1914 (only the files for 1908, 1911 and 1914 are missing). Newly added to the collection, these files are all very large (from 10 to 44,000 KB), and represent an extremely rich set of primary materials for the labor historian.

The third collection contains publications by contemporaries. Here one can find digitized books by leading factory inspectors, Russian and Soviet statisticians, and articles published in specialized journals. We should mention the database that contains bibliographical data on 2,600 articles published in the 1920s and 1930s in the journals *Vestnik truda* and *Voprosy truda*.

The next (fourth) collection includes the most important related publications from Soviet historiography published from the 1930s to the 1980s. Divided into two sections (pre-revolutionary and Soviet), the listings include monographs, chapters in books, articles, and dissertations.

The fifth section contains digital copies of post-Soviet publications (books and articles) that give new interpretations of relations between workers and entrepreneurs, workers' literacy and cultural life, and industrial work incentives in the period under consideration. The section is divided into three parts. The first presents works by Russian scholars (in much greater detail than in our fourth section on historiography), and it is noteworthy that many of these studies have been published since the year 2000, representing a rich research agenda in the field of labor history. The second part lists works by colleagues participating in the labor history project represented by this TOHIR, including (besides the authors of this report) S. V. Ashmarina, A. Iu. Volodin, I. M. Garskova, Iu. I. Kir'ianov, A. V. Miriasov, and E. I. Safonova. The third part contains four citations by foreign scholars.

The bibliography of the TOHIR (sixth section) presents more than 4,500 titles of related books and articles.

The seventh section is a set of databases on the dynamics of workers' wages and occupations in different branches of Russian industry, as well as the dynamics of food prices (data collected from both archival sources and publications). All databases are provided with detailed explanations and references to sources.

The next section contains images of digitized archival and other documents taken mostly from personal and family archives (such as a diploma given for graduation from a primary factory school in 1913). Researchers will find images of reports by OGPU (secret service) agents about the political mood of workers at a large plant in Leningrad (1925), and images of GULAG administration documents dating from the 1930s.

The ninth collection consists from digitized copies of archival documents taken from federal, Moscow and regional archives as well as from issues of Soviet newspapers published in the 1920s and 1930s. This section contains documents on workers' protests in the 1920s. The social policy of Russian entrepreneurs during World War I is preserved in a collection of factory announcements (about 100 of them are presented on the website).

The next section includes collections of graphic materials that include the following varieties of information: photographs of the everyday life of workers, workers' awards from the beginning of the twentieth century and during early Soviet times, and relevant posters and maps. Examples of featured materials include images of the Iaroslavl' Great Factory and the Prokhorovskaia Factory in the Moscow region, and a lengthy listing of Soviet posters on the history of labor dating from 1917 to 1935.

The last part of our TOHIR presents a collection of more than 300 references to relevant Internet resources at other websites (both in Russia and abroad).

In sum, by July, 2006, the total number of files mounted on the TOHIR section of the website was about 500. They occupy about two gigabytes of memory. The number of visits in 2005-2006 amounted to more than 15.000, indicating a considerable degree of scholarly and educational interest shown by researchers in these topically-oriented materials.

NOTES

1. The URL (English page) of the Faculty of History at Moscow State University is http://www.hist.msu.ru/ER/English/index.htm.
2. The URL for the English version of the Electronic Library (three main sections) is http://www.hist.msu.ru/ER/Etext/index_e.html; the URL for the Russian version (12 main sections) is http://www.hist.msu.ru/ER/Etext/index.html.

3. The Book of Veles is said to be a text of ancient Slavic religion. It was supposedly discovered in 1919 and lost in 1941. But it has been proved to be a forgery written in the 1940s or early 1980s.

4. More details are given in the following publication: L. I. Borodkin and I. M. Garskova, "Information Resources on the History of Labor Relations in Russian Industry" (in Russian), *Ekonomicheskaia istoriia: obozrenie* 11 (2006): 8-25.

doi:10.1300/J167v08n02_08

Russia Beyond Russia Digital Library: History, Concept, and Development

Nadia Zilper
Rita Van Duinen

SUMMARY. In this article we share our experience in building the Core Module of the *Russia Beyond Russia* Digital Library (RBR), funded by the Andrew W. Mellon Foundation. We explore the André Savine Collection, trace the evolution of the RBR digitization project, describe the conceptual models of the RBR and Core Module, and follow the progression of the Core Module development. We also look into future development of the RBR Digital Library. doi:10.1300/J167v08n02_09 *[Article copies available for a fee from The Haworth Document Delivery Service: 1-800-HAWORTH. E-mail address: <docdelivery@haworthpress.com> Website: <http://www.HaworthPress.com> © 2007 by The Haworth Press, Inc. All rights reserved.]*

Nadia Zilper is Curator, Slavic and East European Collections and the André Savine Collection, and Department Head, Global Resources and Area Studies Collection Development, Davis Library, University of North Carolina at Chapel Hill, Chapel Hill, NC 27514-8890 (E-mail: nadia@email.unc.edu).

Rita Van Duinen was Project Librarian, André Savine Collection, Davis Library, University of North Carolina at Chapel Hill, Chapel Hill, NC 27514-8890.

A Russian version of this article was published as "Kornevoi modul' elektronnoi biblioteki 'Rossiia Vne Rossii': istoriia, kontseptsiia i razvitie," *Bibliotechnyi forum Ukrainy* 2006, no. 3, 47-53. The English version appears by permission.

[Haworth co-indexing entry note]: "*Russia Beyond Russia* Digital Library: History, Concept, and Development." Zilper, Nadia, and Rita Van Duinen. Co-published simultaneously in *Slavic & East European Information Resources* (The Haworth Information Press, an imprint of The Haworth Press, Inc.) Vol. 8, No. 2/3, 2007, pp. 95-108; and: *Access to East European and Eurasian Culture: Publishing, Acquisitions, Digitization, Metadata* (ed: Miranda Remnek) The Haworth Information Press, an imprint of The Haworth Press, Inc., 2007, pp. 95-108. Single or multiple copies of this article are available for a fee from The Haworth Document Delivery Service [1-800-HAWORTH, 9:00 a.m. - 5:00 p.m. (EST). E-mail address: docdelivery@haworthpress.com].

Available online at http://seeir.haworthpress.com
© 2007 by The Haworth Press, Inc. All rights reserved.
doi:10.1300/J167v08n02_09

KEYWORDS. Émigré, Russian Diaspora, André Savine, *Russia Beyond Russia*, Russian currency, Bibliophile Russe, antiquarian, White Army

ANDRÉ SAVINE COLLECTION

In the spring of 2002, the University of North Carolina at Chapel Hill acquired a sizable collection of materials on the Russian Diaspora from the widow of André Savine, owner of the Paris antiquarian book dealership Le Bibliophile Russe. Altogether this collection contains over 60,000 items and a number of archives totaling approximately 30,000 pages. Among the treasures are: printed books, journals, and periodicals; hand- and type-written newspapers, journals, books, and other manuscripts; photographs, postcards, sound recordings, and currency. The most valuable part of the collection, and the dearest to André Savine's heart, was a compilation of materials on the history of the Russian White Army abroad that he named "Militaria."

Those specializing in Slavic scholarly materials may remember the exquisite annotated catalogs produced by André Savine. Information for these catalogs was derived from Savine's records, which he kept on approximately 16,000 index cards and 5,500 notebook pages. The Russia Beyond Russia Core Module is based on this material.

EVOLUTION OF THE RUSSIA BEYOND RUSSIA PROJECT (RBR)

In 1999, Nadia Zilper submitted a proposal to the East Coast Consortium of Slavic Libraries (ECC) for the creation of Russia Beyond Russia: a multi-institutional initiative to create a digital library of electronic texts comprised of monographs, serials, and manuscripts, as well as sound recordings and images published by Russians outside of Russia, from the beginning of printing to the present. For a number of reasons, this proposal did not come to fruition at that time.

With the receipt of the André Savine Collection in 2002, we began to think about ways to process it and make valuable and unique material available to as many scholars as possible. The idea of the Russia Beyond Russia digital initiative resurfaced, and work on a conceptual design of the database began. In determining the design and functionalities of the digital library, we envisioned it having Russian-language search and retrieval capabilities, in addition to employing the most current metadata standards for consistent resource description, discovery, navigation, and maintenance. We also wanted users to be able to see the original documents.

We examined ways in which we could unite different parts of the André Savine Collection through indexing. Thus the idea was born to create a modular digital library with a central scalable index hub we call the Core Module. Each RBR module can represent any compilation of documents united by a subject or format. All future RBR modules will be indexed and thus cross-referenced through the Core Module. Scalability of the Core Module insures growth and sustainability of RBR. Figure 1 shows the conceptual model of the *Russia Beyond Russia* Digital Library.

The next step was to determine what materials would be included in the Core Module and how the indexing would be performed. We decided that the Savine index cards and notebook pages were an excellent resource for the foundation of the Core Module. In Figures 2 and 3 are examples of Savine's cards and notebook pages.

Savine's index cards and notebook pages contain bibliographic descriptions of each title in the stock of his bookstore, Le Bibliophile

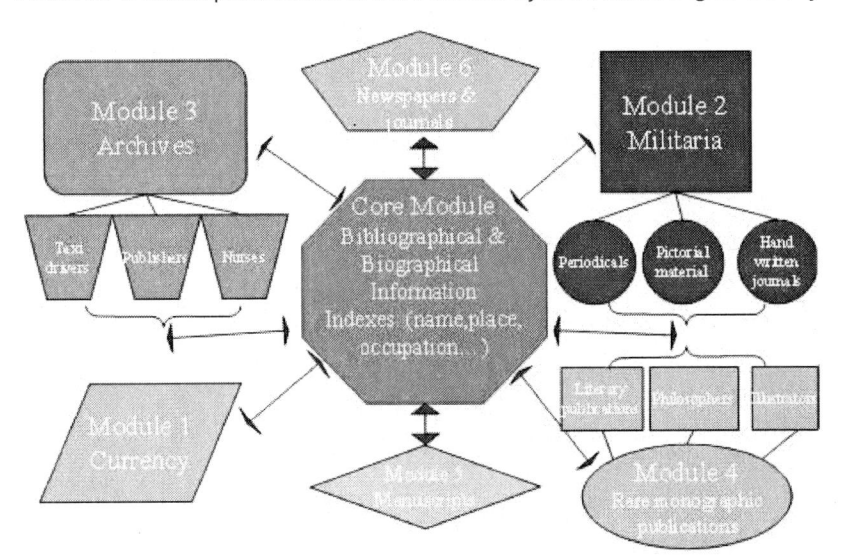

FIGURE 1. Conceptual Model of the *Russia Beyond Russia* Digital Library

FIGURE 2. Example of Savine's Index Cards

> АВРАМОВ П.М. Ковылий сказ. Яровой сев. Париж 1960. Издание " Родимого Края". Стр.84. Повесть о казаках. Бумажная рисованная обложка. 75 ф.
>
> Кат. 30 ① (лит-ра)
>
> К ат. 38 275—
> Предл. Cambridge (11.XII.84)
>
> АВРАМОВ П.М. Ковылий сказ. Яровой сев. Париж 1960. Издание " Родимого Края". Стр. 84. Последние издания, о которых упоминает автор в примечаниях, ТАК НИКОГДА И НЕ ВЫШЛИ. Бумажная обложка. К МАТЕРИАЛАМ ПО ИСТОРИИ РУССКОЙ КУЛЬТУРЫ / РУССКАЯ ЛИТЕРАТУРА В ЭМИГРАЦИИ ЗАБЫТЫЕ ИМЕНА. КАЗАЧЬЯ ЛИТЕРАТУРА/. 275 ф.
>
> Предл. Pleyer (4.I.85) Спец. список N2 (личный)
> Каталог N56 (январь 1985)

FIGURE 3. Example of Savine's Notebook Pages

> **АВРАМОВ П. М.**
> **Ковылий сказ. Яровой сев.**
> Франция (Аньер). 1960. Издание "Родимого Края".
> Стр. 84.
> Формат 18х14 см.
> Тираж 500 экземпляров.
>
> Строгая издательская шрифтовая обложка. Отличная сохранность.
>
> > Первое издание. Автор - донской казак. В предлагаемой книге помещены две короткие повести о жизни казаков на родном для автора Дону. Они описывают природу и казачий быт, свободолюбивый край с его особенностями, с его населением крестьян - воинов, который развивался в системе Русского государства. Все крепкие казачьи традиции, хозяйственность, чувство собственности, преданность казачьему быту, верность семье и сыновнему долгу... - всё это рухнуло с революцией и ушло в прошлое. Предлагаемую книгу можно с полным основанием отнести к жанру мемуарной прозы. Ценный материал по истории России для славистов, историков, библиографов. Редкость (у Фостер не упоминается).
>
> В. Рецензия эпохи. "Часовой". Ноябрь 1961 г. № 426. Стр. 18.
>
> 750 фр. фр.

Russe. Descriptions often contain extensive abstracts and biographical information on authors, illustrators, translators, and sometimes people mentioned in the books. He gathered this information from different sources, such as published bibliographies, newspaper and journal articles, obituaries, and interviews with members of the Russian Diaspora. In many instances Savine also preserved oral histories on his index cards by recording information he received in conversations about famous and ordinary Russian émigrés. In other words, Savine's records are a wealth of information extending far beyond bibliographic description.

At this point we began work on a grant proposal for the creation of the Core Module. In the process of working on the proposal we decided to outsource the creation of the Core Module. After searching for a suitable outsourcing agency, we selected East View Information Services (EVIS) as the most qualified in working with texts in Russian and experienced in creating databases that are both well-designed and large in scale.

THE CORE MODULE PROJECT

The Andrew W. Mellon Foundation awarded us funding for the Core Module project in June 2005. We began work in September 2005. From the beginning it was an exciting, creative, and truly collaborative endeavor between our library and EVIS. The initial task was to set up operational logistics for the project: hire project workers; locate suitable project work space; and purchase and set up equipment.

We created two project teams, one at UNC and another, the EVIS team, in Moscow. On the UNC side, Nadia Zilper serves as principal investigator, and Rita Van Duinen as project manager. We also hired two graduate assistants. The Moscow team is headed by a project manager, and includes the Head of the Data Processing team, and programmers. Kirill Fesenko serves as EVIS's project coordinator from his U.S. office. Our organizational logistics are illustrated in Figure 4.

Project Phases

The Core Module project was designed to be built in phases. The first step in the database development is the research phase, followed by the implementation phase (when the actual building of the Core Module occurs). The final phase is deployment of fully functioning, working versions of all components of the Core Module; system production/use; and installation of the Core Module on a local UNC-Chapel Hill library server.

Project Kick-Off Meeting

In September 2005, Kirill Fesenko, EVIS consultant for the project, visited the library to initiate the research phase of the project. Another goal for

**FIGURE 4
Organizational Logistics**

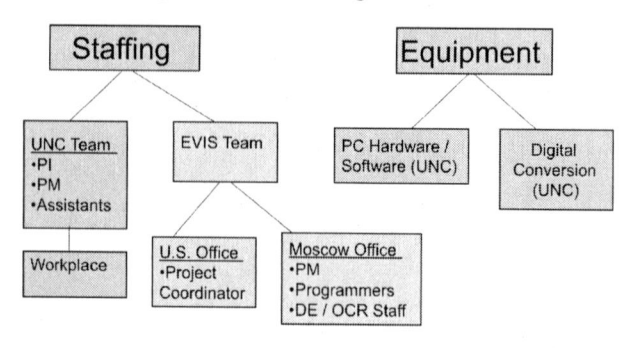

```
                Staffing                        Equipment
       ┌───────────┴───────────┐         ┌──────────┴──────────┐
   UNC Team               EVIS Team   PC Hardware /        Digital
   •PI                                 Software (UNC)       Conversion
   •PM                                                      (UNC)
   •Assistants
       │              ┌────────┴────────┐
   Workplace     U.S. Office      Moscow Office
                 •Project          •PM
                 Coordinator       •Programmers
                                   •DE / OCR Staff
```

the EVIS visit was to host a project kick-off meeting. Our objective in holding this meeting was to consult with as many specialists and potential end users of the system as possible before the concept and details of the Core Module were finalized. For this meeting, we assembled a representative group of librarians, systems staff, and faculty to meet and discuss major themes for the Core Module user interface design and functionality. At the meeting, Fesenko presented a draft concept of the Core Module database, interface prototypes, and proposed functionalities, and asked the group for comments and suggestions. We received valuable suggestions and comments that were incorporated in the design of the database. This was a highly successful and useful meeting.

Design of the Core Module–Research Phase

The research phase is the most important stage of the entire project, during which the design of the whole database is conceptualized, and rules that govern the database and affect its functionality are created. During this phase we accomplished the following tasks: gathering requirements; consulting with specialists and end users; defining technical requirements; identifying criteria for establishing data content and data structures; and setting standards for data entry.

Technical Requirements

In order to begin the research phase for system design and digital conversion, we launched the development of a Technical Requirements paper that provides guidelines for the database application programmers and digital conversion staff. These guidelines contain detailed instructions for the design of the Core Module, including descriptions of user interfaces and functionality, as well as instructions to digital conversion staff.

Data Content and Data Structure

We also set up criteria for establishing data content and data structures of the project materials (index cards and notebook pages). A review of the materials revealed that an individual work is represented by both notebook pages and index cards; or by notebook pages alone; or index cards alone (see Figure 5).

In creating the guidelines for data structuring, we decided that to enhance the usefulness of the project, individual works represented by different sources of information (notebook pages and/or index cards) would be unified by processing and storing all related documents pertaining to that particular work in one Core Module database record.

FIGURE 5

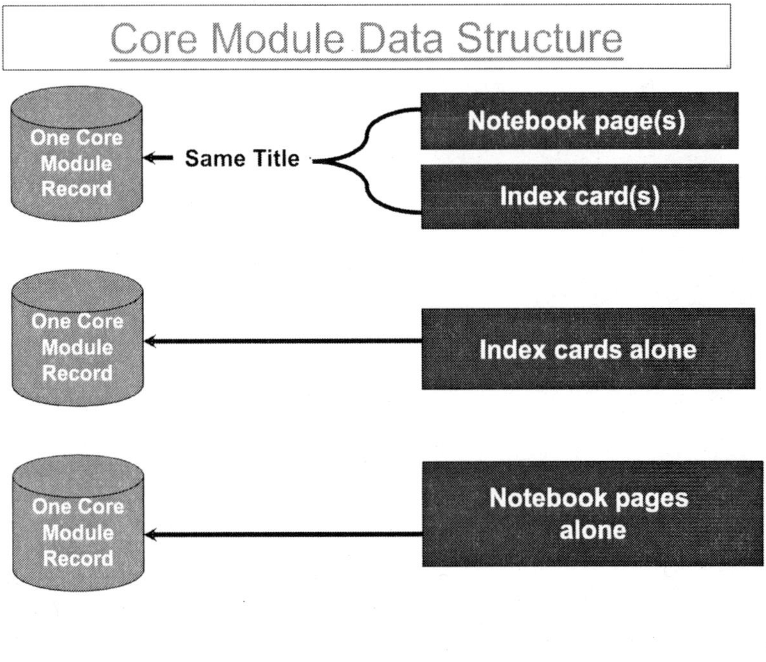

Core Module Data Structure

One Core Module Record ← Same Title — { Notebook page(s) / Index card(s) }

One Core Module Record ← Index cards alone

One Core Module Record ← Notebook pages alone

Data Dictionaries

As part of the technical requirements, the UNC-Chapel Hill project team created data dictionaries for the material being digitized. Data dictionaries outline the rules for indexing and textual conversion, and are an essential component in building the core functionalities of the database. These standards govern the processing and storage of data, digital images, and converted text. Thus data are represented in the database in a consistent manner, resulting in a lower rate of error. While engaged in this phase of planning, project teams corresponded frequently by telephone and e-mail in order to accomplish as much preliminary work as possible before mass production of data began.

Record Display Interface (What the User Will See)

Based on the data structuring requirements we developed, EVIS created a record display interface that provides users with a concise and user-friendly representation of all data associated with a given work. Individual record structures consist of three sections. The first section is labeled *Description* and contains bibliographic information and Savine's annotations. These data are manually entered by the data entry members of the Moscow team. The database search engine will conduct searches in this section. In addition, if Savine's records contain a corresponding title page image for a particular work, its expandable thumbnail image is also displayed in this section.

In the second section, labeled *Related Indexes*, users have access to all index terms and Savine's subject headings followed by a numeric value that represents the number of occurrences of a particular indexed term within the Core Module database. This section also contains the UNC-Chapel Hill copyright statement and the project's "branding" statement, *Russia Beyond Russia*, with a link to the project's website.

The third and final section contains images of Savine's notebook pages and/or index cards for a given work. Users will have the sense of working with an authentic document and will see Savine's handwritten notes, in which he may provide additional information to scholars. To view an example of the records display interface, visit http://online.eastview.com/projects/screens/sample1.html.

Technical Processing Workflow

During the development of the technical requirements, digital conversion of the project materials began at UNC-Chapel Hill in October 2005. The following technical processing workflow procedures for project materials and digital content were developed for the project by both the UNC-Chapel Hill and Moscow teams:

- We created a MS Excel Processing Inventory database for managing the digital imaging, text conversion, and database population portions of the project. This database resides at UNC-Chapel Hill.
- The UNC-Chapel Hill team creates digital images of project materials:
  - Archival TIFF files for local, on-site storage (600 dpi)
  - JPEG working files sent to EVIS (400 dpi)
- The UNC-Chapel Hill team searches every title for WorldCat records. If records are available, we copy and paste them into MS Word and send to EVIS.
- Image files and any accompanying WorldCat records are compressed and sent to EVIS' Moscow office via FTP together with the processing inventory.
- The Moscow team performs the text conversion and data entry.
- The UNC-Chapel Hill team performs quality control once data is processed via the Data Entry Module.

Data Entry Module of the Project

The EVIS Moscow team created the web interface for data entry according to the rules outlined in the Data Dictionaries. The Data Entry Module (DEM) consists of web-based forms used by data entry staff for processing digital images and entering related bibliographic information and annotations from the Savine index cards and notebook pages. The web interface expedites data entry and reduces the possibility of mistakes. It also serves as a quality control tool and provides statistics (weekly, monthly, and annual). The DEM ensures easy access to the data and enables the UNC-Chapel Hill team to review each record as well as perform any necessary updates. Access to the DEM makes it possible for the UNC-Chapel Hill Team to monitor record production by the Moscow team closely. To view an example of the online forms used in the data entry module, visit http://online.eastview.com/projects/screens/input-form.html. Originally the

DEM was not included in the grant proposal. However, once we started working on the project, it became apparent that this module was the best solution for work efficiency.

Browsing by Indexes of the RBR Core Module

The DEM is an integral part in the creation of the Index Module, one of the database searching tools being developed by EVIS. The Index Module incorporates all data processed and entered into the DEM and provides access to information via individual data fields and indexes (see Figure 6). Data in the Index Module will be accessible online to users worldwide long in advance of project completion. The final component in this modular approach to building the database will be the development of the Browsing and Searching Modules, which will access all information in the system and provide relevant search results across all parts of the Core Module. Fully functional browsing by indexes will be available to users at the project site by the end of September 2006 before completion of the project (http://online.eastview.com/projects/savine/index.html). The number of records increases daily as the RBR Core Module is populated.

FIGURE 6

RBR Core Module Indexed Fields

- Author / Автор
- Additional Personal Names / Другие лица
- Place of Publication / Место издания
- Publisher / Издатель
- Date of Publication / Год издания
- Series / Серия
- Print Run / Тираж

- Savine's Subject Headings / Предметные рубрики Савина
- Savine's Geographic Terms / Географические термины Савина
- Organizations / Организации
- Occupation / Род деятельности
- Unique Identifier / Уникальный идентификатор

RESOURCE DISCOVERY ON THE INTERNET, METADATA STRUCTURE

To enhance resource discovery, the UNC-Chapel Hill and EVIS teams have developed sophisticated metadata structures for the project using the Metadata Object Description Schema (MODS), simplified Dublin Core (DC), and the Metadata Encoding Transmission Standard (METS).[1] In the metadata structures we have developed, data fields in the Core Module database will map first to related fields in MODS, then to concurrent fields in simplified DC which will be generated automatically by the database application and exposed for metadata harvesting when queried via the Open Archives Initiative Protocol for Metadata Harvesting (OAI-PMH) by an OAI service provider.[2] METS will be used as a type of "wrapper" or "container" for the metadata output so that the contextual and image structures for each database record are preserved. (See Figure 7.)

Such complex metadata structures ensure the most complete mapping of the project's unique data fields and their content, utilize as many resource discovery tools as possible, and guarantee unfettered access to information in the RBR Core Module database. Moreover, this

FIGURE 7

Metadata Mapping / OAI-PMH Harvesting

metadata mapping / crosswalks: identification of equivalent or nearly equivalent metadata elements within different metadata schemas, used to facilitate the richest semantic representation and interoperability via OAI-PMH harvesting

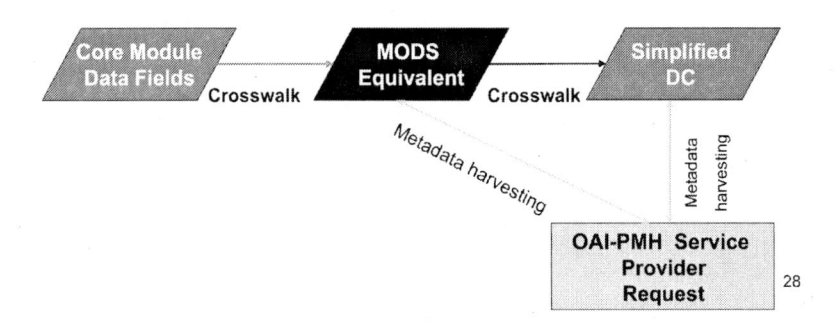

Core Module Data Fields → Crosswalk → MODS Equivalent → Crosswalk → Simplified DC

Metadata harvesting

OAI-PMH Service Provider Request

[28]

metadata schema fosters interoperability across collections and database systems and the scalable design of the Core Module provides for an expandable system.

RESOURCE DISCOVERY THROUGH THE OPAC AND WORLDCAT

Once materials in the André Savine Collection are cataloged, each record in the Core Module database that has a corresponding record in the Library's OPAC will contain a link (via OCLC number) to the Library's cataloging record so that users can easily navigate from the Core Module record to the cataloging record. This will help users locate the original document, see the full cataloging record, and use the Library of Congress subject headings to find related materials outside the Core Module.

Conversely, each OPAC record for materials in the André Savine Collection will also provide users with a direct link to the corresponding record in the Core Module database via a stable URL. UNC-Chapel Hill OPAC records are available in WorldCat, thus users of WorldCat will have direct access to the RBR Core Module. (See Figure 8.)

Since André Savine was an antiquarian book dealer, he sold and traded materials; therefore there are far more cards and notebook pages

FIGURE 8

Resource Discovery through UNC OPAC and WorldCat

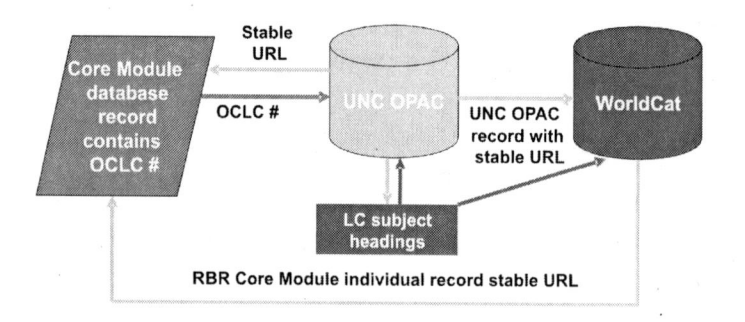

than titles in the André Savine Collection at UNC-Chapel Hill. However, in the interests of scholarly research it would make sense to include stable URLs for all RBR Core Module records in corresponding OCLC records for all the titles that comprise the RBR Core Module. Providing this level of added value would be a special project that could be combined with cataloging the André Savine Collection. Clearly, OCLC's cooperation would be needed for this project.

OVERVIEW OF THE FIRST PHASE OF THE PROJECT

Operational logistics have been set up and effective workflows established. We have conceptualized the Core Module database, determined its functionality, set criteria for data content and structure, and established standards for data entry. We have developed sophisticated metadata structures according to current standards that expose the project metadata to harvesting by all known discovery tools. This metadata schema also ensures easy navigation and sustainability of the database. Moreover, the structure provides compatibility with future RBR modules and supports the functionalities of the future RBR Digital Library. Completion of the RBR Core Module is expected in the fall of 2007. We have provided visibility for the project through Internet presence, presentations, publications, and personal contacts; engaged UNC-Chapel Hill faculty in the project; and satisfied scholarly inquiries for materials in the André Savine Collection.

The RBR Core Module Project Site

The RBR Core Module Project Site can be found at http://online.eastview.com/projects/savine/index.html.

Paper Currency and Bank Notes Database

While unpacking the André Savine Collection we discovered about 600 pieces of paper currency and bank notes, mostly of the Russian Civil War period. We created a database that eventually will become one of the RBR modules. Currently, text is in transliterated form, which in the future will be converted to Cyrillic. See http://www.lib.unc.edu/savine/numismatics/.

NOTES

1. Information on MODS is available at http://www.loc.gov/standards/mods/, on Dublin Core at http://dublincore.org/; on METS at http://www.loc.gov/standards/mets.
2. Information on OAI-PMH is available at http://www.openarchives.org/OAI/openarchivesprotocol.html.

doi:10.1300/J167v08n02_09

Implementing an Image Database for Complex Russian Architectural Objects: The William Brumfield Collection

James D. West
Eileen Llona
Theodore Gerontakos
Michael Biggins

SUMMARY. With support from a National Endowment for the Humanities Reference Materials Program grant for 2006-2008, faculty and librarians at the University of Washington (UW) are collaborating with

---

James D. West, PhD, is Associate Professor, Dept. of Slavic Languages & Literatures, Box 353580, University of Washington, Seattle WA 98195 USA (E-mail: jdwest@u.washington.edu).

Eileen Llona, MLIS, is International Studies Computer Services Librarian, University of Washington Libraries (E-mail: ellona@u.washington.edu).

Theodore Gerontakos, MLIS, is Metadata Librarian for the William Brumfield Russian Architecture Collection, University of Washington Libraries (E-mail: tgis@u.washington.edu).

Michael Biggins, PhD, MS, is Head, Slavic and East European Section, University of Washington Libraries (E-mail: mbiggins@u.washington.edu).

Address correspondence to all three librarians at Box 352900, Seattle WA 98195.

Support for developing the William Brumfield Russian Architecture Collection has been generously provided by the National Endowment for the Humanities, the Gladys Kriebel Delmas Foundation, and the University of Washington Libraries.

[Haworth co-indexing entry note]: "Implementing an Image Database for Complex Russian Architectural Objects: The William Brumfield Collection." West, James D. et al. Co-published simultaneously in *Slavic & East European Information Resources* (The Haworth Information Press, an imprint of The Haworth Press, Inc.) Vol. 8, No. 2/3, 2007, pp. 109-126; and: *Access to East European and Eurasian Culture: Publishing, Acquisitions, Digitization, Metadata* (ed: Miranda Remnek) The Haworth Information Press, an imprint of The Haworth Press, Inc., 2007, pp. 109-126. Single or multiple copies of this article are available for a fee from The Haworth Document Delivery Service [1-800-HAWORTH, 9:00 a.m. - 5:00 p.m. (EST). E-mail address: docdelivery@haworthpress.com].

Available online at http://seeir.haworthpress.com
© 2007 by The Haworth Press, Inc. All rights reserved.
doi:10.1300/J167v08n02_10

William Brumfield (Tulane University) to preserve and catalog the latter's unmatched collection of Russian architectural photographs, create metadata describing the photographs, and make images and text widely accessible as part of an innovative web-based educational and research resource. Building on experience gained through the creation of an experimental pilot database, project staff are adapting emerging standards (METS and CCO) to a custom design that presents images from the Brumfield Collection within their architectural, geographic, and chronological contexts, both as interrelated views of individual structures, and as buildings that share certain structural and stylistic features with other buildings within and beyond the Russian cultural continuum. doi:10.1300/J167v08n02_10 *[Article copies available for a fee from The Haworth Document Delivery Service: 1-800-HAWORTH. E-mail address: <docdelivery@haworthpress.com> Website: <http://www.HaworthPress.com> © 2007 by The Haworth Press, Inc. All rights reserved.]*

KEYWORDS. Image databases, architectural databases, Russian architecture, metadata, METS, William Craft Brumfield, University of Washington Libraries

PROJECT HISTORY

The idea of developing a major online reference collection around William Brumfield's collection of photographs originated in the fall of 2000, when University of Washington (UW) Slavic studies faculty and librarians initiated a series of exploratory conversations with Professor Brumfield.

Over a period of more than three decades, Professor Brumfield has devoted his career at Tulane University to the study of Russian architecture. An indefatigable traveler, skilled and prolific photographer, and inspiring public lecturer, he has not only produced an unrivaled collection of Russian architectural photographs, but has also dedicated himself to the cause of popularizing Russian architecture and art outside of Russia. He has delivered more than 300 public lectures on his specialty at museums, libraries, and universities throughout the United States. Any one of the many thousands of people who have attended his lectures can attest to the revelatory effect of his images viewed on a large screen and accompanied by Professor Brumfield's expert commentary. His photographic prints have been the focus of more than 50 formal exhibits hosted by college, university, and municipal art museums both here and abroad. The National Gallery of Art in Washington, DC, has accessioned a large number of his photographic prints and periodically acquires more, creating what Blair Ruble of the Kennan Institute has characterized as "a major resource [in its own right] for all who study Russia." Ruble goes on to assert that Professor Brumfield's complete collection of Russian architectural photographs, now estimated to number some 100,000 images, "will be viewed a century from now with the same respect and appreciation as we now view the Prokudin-Gorskii Collection [of late-nineteenth- and early twentieth-century Russian photographs] at the Library of Congress . . . . They form a truly remarkable achievement which can enrich future generations' understanding of Russia if properly preserved in digitized form."[1]

The University of Washington's approach to Professor Brumfield coincided with his growing sense of the need for his fragile slides to be preserved from physical deterioration, cataloged, and made available to scholars and teachers for decades to come. A modest grant from the Gladys Kriebel Delmas Foundation made possible a pilot project based on about 1,200 photographs (see Figure 1), which in its turn was instrumental in securing a major grant awarded in 2006 by the Reference Materials Program of the National Endowment for the Humanities. The pilot project used modified Dublin Core as its metadata standard, a custom-designed relational database structure, and an interactive map-based interface to generate integrated screen displays of search results which clustered all interior and exterior views of a given building in a more or less systematic array around an emblematic "key" image of the building's exterior.[2] The experience gained in developing the pilot database led project staff to explore the standards just then emerging for cataloging complex objects, and ultimately to adopt METS (Metadata Encoding and Transmission Standard) and the Visual Research Association's Cataloging Cultural Objects[3] as the encoding and metadata standards for the full-scale project now underway.

SIGNIFICANCE OF THE PROJECT

On completion of the current project, the William Brumfield Russian Architecture Digital Collection will consist of over 30,000 photographs of Russian buildings from the middle ages to the present day, cataloged in detail and with access via an innovative, web-based "smart interface" that facilitates the conversion of images and their descriptions into

FIGURE 1. Main Page of a Pilot Project for the William Brumfield Russian Architecture Collection, Created in 2002-2004

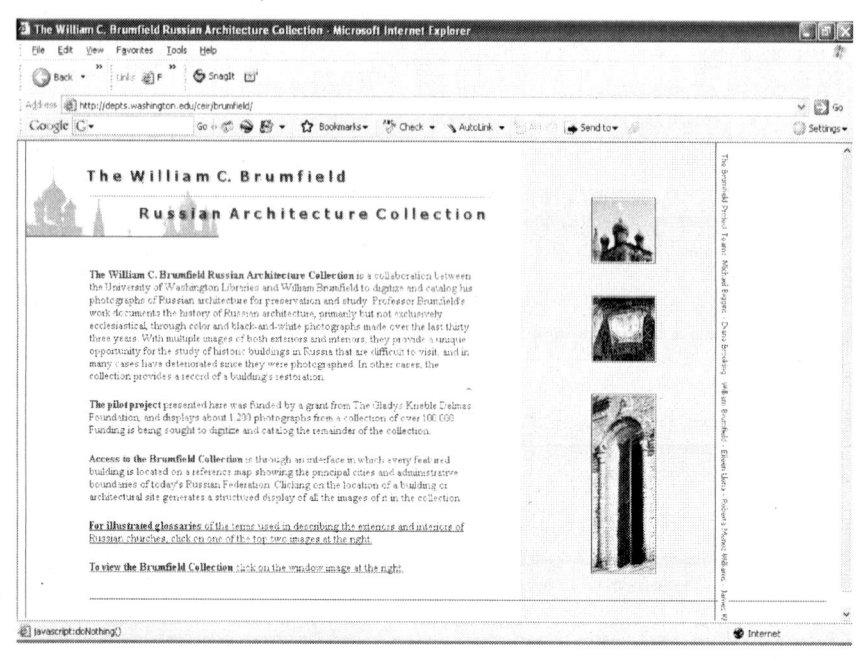

structured information. We expect it will serve for years to come as the primary digital resource for the study of Russian architecture.

Physical access difficulties and a low level of historical preservation over the last hundred years have made architecture a neglected dimension of Russian culture. The number of buildings photographed in the Brumfield collection, the multiple images (up to 50 or more of some architectural objects) including both general views and details of the exteriors and interiors of the most important buildings, the unusually broad range of locations covered and the richness of the descriptive metadata will make access to the collection a virtual visit to architectural sites to which extremely few people are able to travel, including Russian specialists and even most Russians themselves, and will go a long way towards redressing this neglect. A steady decline in the physical state of significant Russian buildings of all periods has heightened the need for a comprehensive record of a disappearing cultural asset, and the Brumfield Collection has additional importance as a body of information that can also support preservation efforts.

As an integrated reference source on Russian architecture, the digital Brumfield Collection as planned has no peers in any format. The relatively few books in English on Russian architecture provide sketchy coverage of the subject, aside from a handful of single-city surveys for a very small number of architecturally rich cities such as St. Petersburg, Novgorod, and Yaroslavl, or regions such as the Russian North (*Architecture of the Russian North, 12th-19th centuries*, edited by B. Fedorov and translated by N. Johnstone, 1976). Even Professor Brumfield's own well-illustrated books–*Landmarks of Russian Architecture: A Photographic Survey* (1997); *Lost Russia: Photographing the Ruins of Russian Architecture* (1995); *An Architectural Survey of St. Petersburg, 1840-1916: Building Inventory* (1994); *A History of Russian Architecture* (1993, enlarged edition 2004); *The Origins of Modernism in Russian Architecture* (1991) contain only a fraction of the images that this project will make available. In Russian, the authoritative series Svod pamiatnikov arkhitektury i monumental'nogo iskusstva Rossii (Collection of Monuments of Architecture and Monumental Art of Russia), begun by the Russian Academy of Sciences in 1997, has so far managed to cover or partially cover only six out of a total of 89 regions in Russia; and, despite the presence of numerous indexes, the print format of the Svod pamiatnikov series at best severely limits the user's ability to bring together and compare buildings with similar attributes, particularly across regional boundaries.

Online resources for Russian architecture are, by comparison with the planned scope of the Brumfield Collection, greatly limited in size and functionality. Even the 1,137 digitized color slides by Professor Brumfield included in the Library of Congress's *Meeting of Frontiers* site are restricted to the Russian North and Western Siberia, provide less rich metadata, and employ a less sophisticated interface. The few open-source databases of Russian architecture that are currently available on the web, while useful for certain purposes, are either too limited in scope or insufficiently focused on the structural aspects of the buildings they display to support research and discovery in Russian architectural history. The admirable *Narodnyi katalog pravoslavnoi arkhitektury* (National Catalog of Orthodox Architecture) is a widely distributed collaborative effort consisting (in spring 2006) of more than 16,000 images with corresponding descriptive text submitted by a host of volunteer contributors from throughout Russia.[4] As its name implies, however, the primary focus of this collection is on architecture as a historical artifact of Russian Orthodoxy, with textual descriptions tending to emphasize a monastery's or a church's role in church or state history over its architectural aspects, little or no attribution of sources, and very little controlled vocabulary for search purposes. The National Catalog is, nonetheless, an impressive effort, not least for some of its auxiliary collaborative features, such as its archived and heavily used online forum for information exchange, and its interactive inventory of missing data, organized by region and building.

Much smaller in scope than the National Catalog, but more expertly designed for architectural study, is the *Katalog pamiatnikov* (Catalog of Monuments) hosted by the website *Arkhitektura Rossii* (Architecture of Russia).[5] Developed by Russian art historians since 1999, the Catalog of Monuments reflects a more deliberately architectural approach to its buildings, each one of which is searchable by building type, date of construction, geographical location, architect (if known) and style. Partly because of its more studied approach and the additional time required to generate controlled metadata, the Catalog of Monuments is more limited in scope, containing in 2006 fewer than 1,000 images of some 300 buildings. The display interface does not allow for complex searches involving Boolean operators, which is not a serious drawback for a small database, but would be badly missed in a much larger one. Finally, and needless to say, the interfaces of both of these valuable databases are in Russian, designed for a Russian audience, and are of only limited use to researchers worldwide.

The audience envisaged for the Brumfield Collection is international in scope, and includes specialists in Russian art and architecture, students of Russia throughout the spectrum of education from high school to graduate school and non-specialist faculty, professionals in fields ranging from architecture to the travel industry, and the public at large. At the broadest possible level, the completed Brumfield Collection will make systematic access to vast quantities of visual and text information about Russian architecture readily available to the English-speaking public for the first time, enabling many hundreds of thousands of members of the general public–from schoolchildren at all levels to art and architecture enthusiasts and travelers preparing for vacation–to discover and develop an appreciation for the elegance, intricacy, and distinctive beauty of the Russian architectural heritage.

The strongest and most urgent needs for the Brumfield Collection site are in two areas: college-level education and research, and historical documentation to support preservation efforts. The physical condition of many of Russia's older buildings, whether ecclesiastical or secular, and the effects on them of ill-informed restoration efforts, give a compelling urgency to the task of providing this accessible historical record.

Although the immediate aim of the current project is to make a significant part of the Brumfield Collection into a definitive, fully functional and self-contained online reference work for the study of Russian architecture, we see the larger project as developing indefinitely in several respects:

- Professor Brumfield will continue to provide the project with new visual material as he photographs new sites, and re-photographs sites he has already visited, since the record of the state of preservation or restoration of buildings over time is an important component of the information in this resource. As individual buildings represented in the collection are restored or deteriorate, and as new information about their history comes to light, there will be a need for continued elaboration and supplementation of the metadata, and additional photographs of sites already covered.
- As web browsers, display technology, programming languages and metadata standards evolve, the programming team will continue to make the Brumfield Collection interface more sophisticated, and may develop a generalized version useful for similar projects.
- There will be an ongoing need for long-term preservation of the digitized images, an area in which the relevant technologies are likely to develop considerably in coming years.

The role of the project in documenting Russian historical buildings for preservation adds a new dimension to the project's urgency: preservation of historical architecture is a process requiring not only the best possible information about buildings, but informed policy decisions at various levels based on a careful evaluation of both their historical significance and their present condition. Russia is already losing historical buildings at an alarming rate, not just to neglect, but to unscrupulous development and even to accident and arson, as vividly documented by Professor Brumfield in recent photographs. It is realistic to assume that the existence of the Brumfield Collection resource will greatly facilitate the engagement of entities outside Russia, such as UNESCO, in a world-wide effort to arrest the deterioration of this precious architectural heritage. Last but not least, the project will preserve a collection that consists at present largely of slide transparencies, many of them already 20 or 30 years old, and housed in a city that came alarmingly close to destruction in the 2005 hurricane season–a fact which adds a further layer of urgency to the digitization component of the project.

OBJECTIVES OF DATABASE DESIGN

When the project is completed, approximately 30,000 slides and photographic prints will have been digitized as both high-resolution archival TIFF images and medium-resolution JPEG images. The latter, with their related catalog information, will be made available for study, at various levels of detail and sophistication, as an extensive web resource housed on a dedicated server, using a custom interface that provides flexible access in a form appropriate to both the nature of the material and the needs of those who will be consulting it. The interface is designed to be a true "information interface," rather than a simple data retrieval system. Access to TIFF images will be provided in a password-protected sector of UW's digital repository for researchers requiring the higher resolution and detail they can provide.

Photographic documentation of buildings and monuments in general requires, as a minimum, a view of all sides of the object and, in the case of buildings, the principal interior spaces. Full documentation requires many more views from different angles, both exterior and interior, and close-up views of details of particular interest. In the field of architectural history, many aspects and features of buildings have become conventional subjects of study in their own right, ranging from particular types of detail and substructures to the interaction between a building and its natural or built environment. Additional aspects of the study of historical buildings are defined by geographical area, period and style.

In the Brumfield Collection, up to 25 to 50 views of each of the most important buildings are provided, ranging from panoramic views of the building in its landscape and architectural environments, to close-up photographs of architectural details, ornamentation and frescoes. A high proportion of Russian ecclesiastical buildings, and Russian buildings of some other types, both in cities and on country estates, are compound architectural entities, consisting of a main building and a group of associated structures. Such entities conventionally carry the name that attaches to the principal building (the largest, or best-known, or most historically significant). A close group of such entities is generally regarded by Russians as an entity in its own right, an *arkhitekturnyi ansambl'* (architectural ensemble) with its own name, often distinct from the names of its component buildings. Lastly, Russia is a physically vast territory, and its architecture has reflected a great variety of regional differences, ranging from local building materials to the influence of the architectural styles of neighboring territories and cultures.

The images of the Brumfield Collection project are cataloged using a metadata set that has been specially devised to describe the most important characteristics of Russian buildings; this metadata set will naturally continue to grow as the bulk of the collection is cataloged. Conventional metadata of this type serve a basic archival purpose, enabling the partial retrieval of stored data based on certain characteristics rather than others. However, for a collection of data that contains groups of interrelated items–in this case, multiple images of different components, features, and directional views of the same building–the most common type of retrieval, based on one or more search criteria with the results displayed sequentially, does not necessarily result in the most intelligent presentation of the material to the user, or the most effective way of revealing the information the material contains. Sequential presentation of search results would not make the interrelations that exist within the material immediately apparent, and the user would need to extrapolate them from displayed metadata.

For the purposes of designing an effective, information-rich interface, the Brumfield Collection material can be viewed as having two types of structure, one that is inherent in virtually any cataloged collection of items with multiple characteristics, and another that reflects both the characteristics of architectural material in general and Russian architecture in particular, and the ways in which architectural objects are conventionally organized for study:

- A structure that is a subset of the data having particular interest for a given user at a given time: the result of a search applying any permutation of constraints drawing on the metadata categories used in describing the architectural entities in the collection;
- A hierarchical structure based on the type of view represented by each image of the same architectural entity. The images may be of:
    - Panoramic scenes that include buildings in their natural or architectural environments.
    - Architectural complexes consisting of several buildings
    - Individual buildings, whether simple or composite, viewed from the exterior or the interior
    - Sub-structures of composite buildings, viewed from the exterior or the interior
    - Details of construction and decoration, both exterior and interior

The information contained in each image goes beyond the detailed physical description of the architectural entity or detail depicted, and includes its place in each of these structures. Although the individual building is at the mid-point rather than the head of the larger conceptual hierarchy and the collection's inherent data structure, it makes sense for several reasons to make the building the entity that is cataloged, and the point of access for information relating to it that is both more general and more specific than the building. In effect, this approach relates all the images in the collection and gives them a meaning that exceeds their individual descriptions.

Besides reflecting the nature of the material, an optimal method of making the visual and verbal information contained in the Brumfield Collection available to the user needs to:

- Reflect the fact that the images in the collection are related in the way described above, and that these group relationships need to be visible to the user if the images displayed in response to a search are to convey the maximum amount of information;
- Supplement the display of search results with additional information that the user will need in order to interpret them, e.g., geographic locations and architectural terminology;
- Provide textual metadata fully adequate to describe each architectural feature or detail displayed, while providing direct access to non-redundant metadata describing the larger architectural context (building or complex) to which they belong;
- To the extent possible, provide a visual presentation of information such as geographic location that is not a part of the images themselves;
- Achieve a compromise between two different means of data access—focused conditional searching and browsing—that are equally productive of interpretable information;
- Display search results in a form that can be manipulated on the computer screen to facilitate their use, including their combination with displays from other applications.

For the purposes of the Brumfield Collection interface design, there is a case for regarding information on the geography and dating of the cataloged objects of Russian architecture as distinct spatial and temporal structures in their own right. The location and date of construction will obviously accompany the display of any image as strictly verbal information, but unlike the rest of the descriptive metadata, this information would not have a visible counterpart in the images. The Brumfield Collection interface makes this information more easily assimilated, and the patterns that underlie it more clearly revealed, by situating the buildings that meet the user's search criteria within a detailed map context that also lends itself to chronological groupings of search results.

IMAGING STANDARDS

High quality scans of more than 16,000 prints and color slides targeted for the project have been produced using a slide scanner. Scanning of the remaining 14,000 images is being contracted out to a commercial vendor. To ensure the usefulness of the resulting digital collection for future generations, standardized imaging practices have been implemented whenever possible. To determine project specifications for scanning, literature was surveyed, an experienced digitization specialist was hired by the project, project staff discussed final specifications, and Professor Brumfield approved and augmented the specifications as needed.[6]

Professor Brumfield is doing much of the scanning himself and, as the photographer and owner of the images, is able to lend his authority to improving the digitization process. Brumfield ensures fidelity to the original photos using digital filters and dynamic range adjustments–processes that are omitted from project specifications and prohibited to all digitizers except Professor Brumfield. Other digitizers *are* expected to contribute to the project, as nearly 50% of the digitization will be outsourced to a digitization professional in New Orleans. The resulting digital images, all in TIFF file format, are stored on magnetic hard drives.

Professor Brumfield reviews every image. During this process he adds image information (metadata), including a file name based on filing practices of the original slide collection, the name of the work (i.e., building) depicted, its geographic location, and brief comments on particularly notable aspects of the building or any details depicted. Files are grouped in directories representing geographic regions in Russia, which are transferred to the University of Washington via FTP. At UW, images received by the FTP server are itemized in a receiving log, then transferred to a permanent home on a local server, which is backed up on a regular basis. Derivative files are then produced from these master images, including JPEGs (resized, cropped, slightly adjusted, and sharpened derivatives) for use on the project website. Every image, TIFF and JPEG, is reviewed at UW for quality assurance.

At 4000 ppi, 35 mm slides yield scans that are about 4000 x 5900 pixels with file sizes of about 20 MB for Grayscale with LZW compression, approximately 40 MB for RGB with LZW. Without LZW compression the images are almost 50% larger (30 MB grayscale/60 MB RGB).[7] Selected project specifications for master digital images are summarized in Table 1. Table 2 summarizes selected project specifications for web-display derivative images as of the date of this writing.

METADATA RESEARCH, CREATION AND CONTROLLED VOCABULARIES

Based on a metadata scheme specially designed to accommodate the needs of retrieving and collocating Russian architectural images, the Brumfield Collection's array of user access points and descriptive text is designed to be easily mastered by a wide range of users, while it remains respectful of the many subtleties and factual details that are crucial for accurate documentation of these objects.

TABLE 1. Summary of Selected Project Specifications for Master Digital Images

Devices anticipated	Nikkon Super Coolscan 8000 ED; Kodak Professional HR 500 Plus
Input resolution	4000 ppi
Bit depth, color	24-bit RGB
Bit depth, b&w	8-bit grayscale
File type	TIFF 6.0
Compression	None; LZW is admissible, however, and will be used by Professor Brumfield

TABLE 2. Summary of Selected Project Specifications for Web-Display Derivative Images (as of This Date Still Subject to Change)

Compression	JPEG
Photo editing software	Adobe Photoshop
Editing procedure 1	Crop slide mount
Editing procedure 2	Resize: 710 H or 990 W, whichever comes first
Editing procedure 3	Histogram: restrict dynamic range to actual image information
Editing procedure 4	Histogram: slight mid-tone adjustment, if needed
Editing procedure 5	Unsharp Mask Filter, Amount=75 or 100, Radius=1.0, Threshold=1
Editing procedure 6	Save as JPEG, quality Level 3

Two part-time research assistants with superior Russian-language skills consult a range of authoritative print and online sources, nearly all of them in Russian, to gather supplementary information about individual buildings and their features beyond the initial information provided by Prof. Brumfield, focusing on data that supports completion of the project's array of metadata fields. The research assistants then enter this information in English into a custom view of the project's Microsoft Access data entry interface, leaving much in narrative form, while entering only a few specific categories of information (such as dates of construction and renovation) in formatted fields of the data entry form that generate appropriate METS file encoding. Once all available relevant inform- ation is recorded, the research assistants save the new work record and tag it for review by the project's metadata librarian. Working from a separate, final stage view of the data entry interface (see Figures 2 and 3)–one that prompts consistently for controlled vocabulary input– the metadata librarian then converts raw text into formal metadata, using an array of metadata fields and thesauri as recommended by the Visual Resource Association's *Cataloging Cultural Objects*. A record status field allowing for a range of values enables project staff to tag each work record for its current stage in the research and cataloging process.

Name headings, for both buildings and persons (architects, notable inhabitants or owners, etc.), are established according to the *Anglo-American Cataloging Rules*, 2nd edition, revised (AACR2rev), which stipulates that name headings be established in the vernacular language–here, Russian transliterated into Roman characters according to the Library of Congress transliteration system. Additionally, the Brumfield Collection metadata scheme provides for a secondary, English-language name heading for buildings, for which the project catalogers generate an accurate English translation of the standard Russian form of name (heading). The metadata scheme also retains the capability for the later inclusion of a third variant heading for building names: Russian in Cyrillic script.

For topical access, the project uses the Getty *Art and Architecture Thesaurus* (AAT), which of all available thesauri has proven most suited to describing this subject. But the AAT is generally oriented toward highly detailed description of Western rather than Russian art and architecture. Brumfield project cataloging staff are generating a number of new, Russian-specific headings to supplement the AAT's

FIGURE 2. Initial Fields of the Final-Stage (Metadata Librarian's) View of the William Brumfield Russian Architecture Collection's Metadata Entry Form, Designed to Produce a METS-Encoded Output File for Each Work (or Building) in the Collection

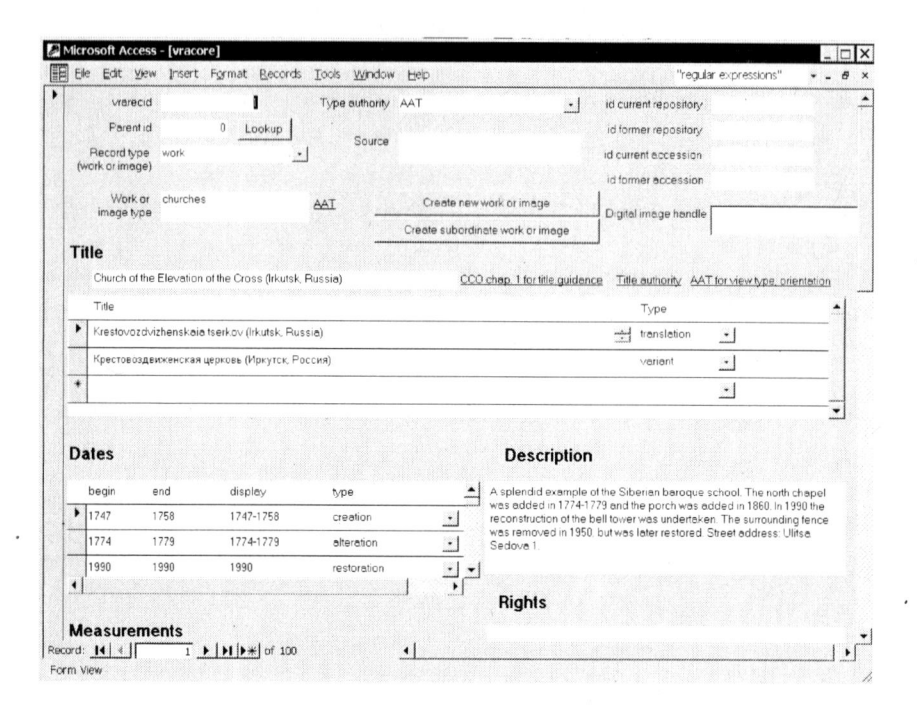

repertory of terms, particularly for uniquely Russian architectural features, techniques, and styles. Project staff have submitted some of these new headings to the AAT's editorial staff to consider for inclusion in future editions of the thesaurus, but for purposes of the Brumfield Collection they are immediately operational.

Topical access through the collection's interface will be through a hierarchy of terms, taking the user from broad, intuitive topical category choices to the specific AAT-based headings used as archival metadata. An illustrated online glossary of architectural and art terms is designed to familiarize users with the terminology employed at this level of architectural description, and will fill a significant gap among currently available reference resources by providing an extensive Russian-English and English-Russian glossary of architectural terms.

FIGURE 3. Remaining Fields of the Metadata Librarian's View of the Brumfield Russian Architecture Collection Metadata Entry Form

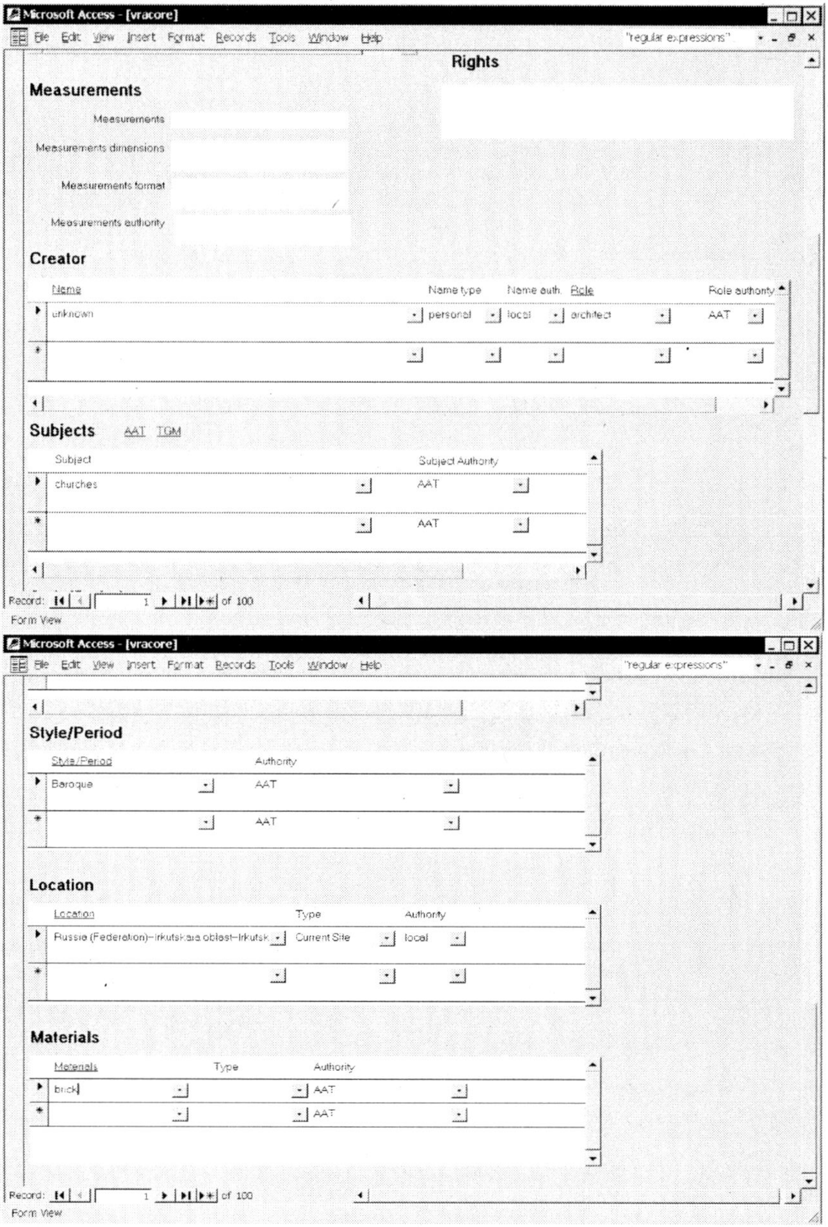

METADATA ENCODING

The current plan for delivering the images to users involves the use of web-based technologies, including Geographic Information Systems (GIS), and server-side and client-side scripting technologies, with the goal of making each image's metadata fully searchable and displayable. However, we realize that presentation technologies will continue to evolve, and that in order to take advantage of future methods for presentation, the underlying metadata need to be in a flexible yet secure format for preservation. Current best practices for metadata structures utilize XML-based schemas, such as those endorsed by the Library of Congress; examples include the Metadata Object Description Standard (MODS) and the Metadata Encoding and Transmission Standard (METS). Using XML-based standards for the project's underlying metadata will allow for flexibility in continuing the development of the current GIS-based interface. The use of structured metadata schemas for modeling complex data relationships, such as those found in architectural collections, has the advantage of providing a standardized, documented format that can be transferred to any suite of delivery and presentation mechanisms. It also should help to minimize redundancies in cataloging, and allow clearer relationships to be described between the architectural components, regardless of the presentation format. Through this work, project staff expect to contribute to the knowledge of documenting complex architectural works and features using hierarchical metadata schemas, a process that is still in the early stages of its evolution and where standards for certain situations have yet to be developed.

Formatting of metadata as METS documents is facilitated by a server-side relational database (Microsoft SQL Server), with Microsoft Access being used for the client-based data entry forms described above. Technical metadata from the images are extracted and incorporated into the METS documents. From this point, data from the METS documents can be extracted and incorporated into the interface.

STORAGE, MAINTENANCE, AND PROTECTION OF DATA

The technologies used for making the Brumfield collection available over the web require extensive server-side CPU and memory capacity and a suite of server-side software tools that are dependent on particular hardware and version configurations. These technologies make minimal hardware and software demands on users' computers (whether PC, Mac, or Unix), so that any computer with a 56K or higher Internet connection and a web browser (Internet Explorer 4.0 + , Netscape 6.0 + , and other post-2002 browsers) can gain optimal access to the resource. As the site grows to accommodate more information, both in terms of images and geographic layers, we anticipate that the load on the server-based software will increase. Hence, we may need higher-end server technology to provide the spatial and image resources. Server upgrades will be made and storage space augmented as the project progresses. While we plan to use UW-based storage space, we anticipate requiring backup and on-demand space for the less frequent use of the high-resolution preservation images that the project will generate.

Though the primary objective of this project is to provide the widest possible access to the photographic material of the Brumfield Collection, the long-term success of the project, given its longevity and the necessary assumption of continued development for an indefinite future, is conditional on secure storage of the digitized images on which it is based. The original slides will remain the property of William Brumfield or his heirs. In addition to possession of the original slides, negatives, and prints, Professor Brumfield will continue to hold copyright to the digital images, but has granted UW the appropriate rights to use the digital images as part of the Brumfield Collection. UW will be responsible for storing the digitized images on appropriate media, and maintaining this store in a computing environment in which mass storage technology, both hardware and software, is rapidly evolving. Initially, the approximately 800 gigabytes of freely accessible Brumfield materials will be housed on a UW Libraries server using the same industry-standard back-up technology that supports UW Libraries catalogs and collections, and stored on appropriate physical media in a secure location free from electrical interference and away from the worksite.

As the project proceeds, the Brumfield Collection technical team will be working in close consultation with the experimental UW-based Digital Well project, which is developing innovative solutions to the problems of cataloging, storing, delivering, and managing large collections of digital content, and enabling access to high quality, high definition video and audio materials via Internet2 networks. In mid-June 2003, Digital Well deployed a Topspin Communications 360 InfiniBand-based switched computing system in support of the university's digital video media library to provide high-bandwidth, low-latency connectivity within the university's Intel-based streaming media server clusters, and between these clusters and their Fibre Channel SANs for digital video archives, as well as Ethernet LANs for connectivity to clients. The Digital Well is closely associated with both the UW Computing and Communications Advanced Systems and Technologies Group and the UW Libraries Archives Division; and our consulting relationship will ensure that the systems developed for the Brumfield Collection project are integrated into, and fully interoperable with, the UW Libraries' campus-wide and off-campus developments in digital information storage and access.

NOTES

1. Blair Ruble, personal letter dated February 2005.
2. The pilot database is available at http://depts.washington.edu/ceir/brumfield/. Pop-up blockers should be disabled for successful display of search results.
3. See the METS home page (http://www.loc.gov/standards/mets) and the CCO home page (http://www.vraweb.org/ccoweb/).
4. For the Library of Congress site, see http://lcweb2.loc.gov/intldl/mtfhtml/mfdigcol/mfdcphot.html#a. For the National Catalog of Orthodox Architecture, see http://www.sobory.ru/.
5. For the Catalog of Monuments, see http://www.archi.ru/.
6. Many of these resources are available online at present, including:

- *Western States Digital Imaging Best Practices*, version 1.0, January 2003, http://www.cdpheritage.org/digital/scanning/documents/WSDIBP_v1.pdf.
- United States National Archives and Records Administration, *Technical Guidelines for Digitizing Archival Materials for Electronic Access: Creation of Production Master Files–Raster Images*, June 2004, written by Steve Puglia, Jeffrey Reed, and Erin Rhodes, http://www.archives.gov/research/arc/digitizing-archival-materials.pdf.
- *Recommendations for Digitizing for RLG Cultural Materials*, http://www.rlg.org/en/page.php?Page_ID=220.
- *A Framework for Building Good Digital Collections*, 2nd ed., 2004, http://www.niso.org/framework/Framework2.html.
- *The NINCH Guide to Good Practice in the Digital Representation and Management of Cultural Heritage Materials*, http://www.nyu.edu/its/humanities/ninchguide/.

7. LZW compression (Lempel-Ziv-Welch) is a lossless data compression algorithm published in 1984. It is the basis of the GIF file format.

doi:10.1300/J167v08n02_10

Digitizing the Zdenka and Stanley B. Winters Collection of Czech and Slovak Posters, 1920-1991

Patricia Hswe

SUMMARY. Donated to the University of Illinois at Urbana-Champaign in the early 1990s, the Zdenka and Stanley B. Winters Collection of Czech and Slovak Posters, 1920-1991, consists of nearly 500 posters that address a range of subjects, including architecture, art, folklore, literature, music, nature, politics, sports, technology, theater, and tourism. This paper describes a project by UIUC's Slavic and East European Library to digitize the collection. It provides some background about the posters and details the steps taken toward making them more accessible via their digital images. doi:10.1300/J167v08n02_11 *[Article copies available for a fee from The Haworth Document Delivery Service: 1-800-HAWORTH. E-mail address: <docdelivery@haworthpress.com> Website: <http://www.HaworthPress.com> © 2007 by The Haworth Press, Inc. All rights reserved.]*

Patricia Hswe, PhD, was the 2004-2006 CLIR Slavic Digital Humanities Fellow in the Slavic and East European Library, University of Illinois at Urbana-Champaign. At present she is enrolled in the Graduate School of Library and Information Science at UIUC.

Address correspondence to: Patricia Hswe, PhD, Graduate School of Library & Information Science, 501 E. Daniel Street, MC-493, Champaign, IL 61820-6211 USA (E-mail: phswe@uiuc.edu).

[Haworth co-indexing entry note]: "Digitizing the Zdenka and Stanley B. Winters Collection of Czech and Slovak Posters, 1920-1991." Hswe, Patricia. Co-published simultaneously in *Slavic & East European Information Resources* (The Haworth Information Press, an imprint of The Haworth Press, Inc.) Vol. 8, No. 2/3, 2007, pp. 127-136; and: *Access to East European and Eurasian Culture: Publishing, Acquisitions, Digitization, Metadata* (ed: Miranda Remnek) The Haworth Information Press, an imprint of The Haworth Press, Inc., 2007, pp. 127-136. Single or multiple copies of this article are available for a fee from The Haworth Document Delivery Service [1-800-HAWORTH, 9:00 a.m. - 5:00 p.m. (EST). E-mail address: docdelivery@haworthpress.com].

Available online at http://seeir.haworthpress.com
© 2007 by The Haworth Press, Inc. All rights reserved.
doi:10.1300/J167v08n02_11

KEYWORDS. University of Illinois, posters, graphic design, digitization, Czech, Slovak, culture

INTRODUCTION

In late 1991 the University of Illinois at Urbana-Champaign (UIUC) became the new home for an eclectic collection of Central European posters dating from the early to the late twentieth century. The Zdenka and Stanley B. Winters Collection of Czech and Slovak Posters, 1920-1991, consists of nearly 500 posters, which address a range of subjects, including architecture, art, folklore, literature, music, nature, politics, sports, technology, theater, and tourism.[1] The posters feature original graphic design by such artists as Adolf Born, Cyril Bouda, Josef Flejšar, Vratislav Hlavatý, Milan Kodejš, Čestmír Pechr, and Karel Teissig, several of whom have won awards for their art. This article provides information about the Winters and their interest in poster collecting; a discussion highlighting particular treasures of the collection; and a detailed description of efforts made by the Slavic and East European Library (http://www.library.uiuc.edu/spx/) and the Digital Services and Development Unit (http://images.library.uiuc.edu/) to digitize the collection to make it more accessible for faculty and student researchers.[2]

A PASSION FOR POSTERS

It was a gift from a Slovak colleague that first sparked the interest of Stanley B. Winters in posters. In 1967, Dr. Winters, a former professor of history at the New Jersey Institute of Technology, was in Bratislava for a meeting of historians and received a present of several posters from his friend, who was in the Slovak capital for the same meeting. The colors and creativity of the posters' graphic design especially intrigued Dr. Winters. His wife, Zdenka Winters, as a native Czech, long had known the powerful communicative effects of posters, which typically are on prominent display in the streets of European cities. This sensibility, along with Mrs. Winters's experience as a career librarian and her enthusiasm for the visual arts, as well as Dr. Winters's affinity for intellectual history and politics (he is an author and editor of several books on these topics)[3], stood the couple in good stead as they began collecting from the late 1960s onward. Their visits to museums of almost every kind, to castles and other sightseeing destinations, to concerts and festivals, and to events marking special anniversaries resulted in a collection of notable diversity. In fewer than 20 years they had amassed enough items to exhibit a part of their collection. As the finding aid to the collection states, the exhibit was held at the Newark Public Library in 1981 and may well have been the first of its kind (a display of only Czech and Slovak posters) to have occurred in the United States up to that point.

When the time came to decide where the collection should be housed permanently, Dr. and Mrs. Winters considered the University of Illinois, where the professor had been an associate of the Summer Research Laboratory of the Russian and East European Center (now known as the Russian, East European, and Eurasian Center, or REEEC). It turns out that he had another connection with UIUC: in the early 1940s, as a young military draftee, he was sent to the university to take courses in mathematics in preparation for the Army Specialized Training Program, or ASTP. Furthermore, the Winters chose the University of Illinois because of its renowned collection of Central and East European materials and because of the expertise and high level of service shown regularly by the staff of the Slavic and East European Library. The couple wanted to make their posters available to scholars and, as a major research institution with world-class holdings, the University of Illinois made a sound choice in every respect.

COLLECTION HIGHLIGHTS

The Winters Collection comprises 488 posters, organized in 26 folders containing approximately 20 posters each and categorized according to subject matter.[4] The posters came to the University of Illinois in excellent condition overall. The almost pristine state of the collection attests to the Winters' careful attention to the handling and storage of the posters prior to the donation, considering in particular that the quality of paper during the Soviet era, when most of the items in the collection were published, was substandard. The categorical distribution of the posters is as follows: Artistic (six folders); Individual Artists, Personalities (two folders); Alphonse Mucha (two folders); Tourist, Nature, and Political (four folders); Technical (two folders); Children (one folder); Folk Art (four posters), and Cultural and Political (four folders). Although the range of the collection is given as 1920 to 1991, the bulk of the posters date from the 1970s and 1980s.

The collection offers many examples of innovative contemporary graphic design from Central Europe. One subset of such posters consists of advertisements for theatrical productions. Three of these (posters no. 24, 25, and 26) were created by the team Brom/Kopřiva to publicize various dramatic stagings, such as plays by Sophocles and Alfred de Musset, at the experimental workshop theater Divadlo za Branou (Theater beyond the Gate) in Prague in the late 1960s and early 1970s. The artwork on the posters iconically represents what the plays are about. For example, the piece that advertises a production of Sophocles's *Oedipus Rex* shows a face made of stone, with dark chasms where the eyes should be and the mouth agape as if in horror, all of which betray the hero's despair and precipitous fall from virtue. Another theatrical poster, this one designed by Čestmír Pechr and dating from the same era as those produced by Brom/Kopřiva, was for a staging of William Shakespeare's tragedy *Richard II* (poster 75). It has an illustration of two hands, made of maggot-like fingers, that seem to be covering a face out of despair; but there is no face visible through the spaces between the fingers–there is only a black space, like an abyss–while above the fingers is a crown. All of this suggests a monarch whose reign is a sham, held up by base deeds and dark ambition. The only other Pechr poster in the Winters Collection is a work the artist painted for a production titled *Julie, ty más nápady!* (Julie, What Ideas You Have!), and it could not be more different in style and design from the *Richard II* poster. The *Julie* poster (no. 42), created some years before the one for *Richard II,* is reminiscent of a collage: Pechr uses textured fabrics such as lace for the contours of a woman's profile in a hat and high-necked blouse, with her earrings dangling. The result is a portrait of sophistication in various shades of gray against a white background. While it is true that the plays from which Pechr designed these posters diverge radically in plot-hence, in part, the stylistic differences between the art on the posters–a researcher specializing in Central European graphic design or in the work of Pechr himself may be interested in examining them more closely to see if *anything* is discernibly "Pechrian" about them, and if not, then why. There are other similar instances in the Winters Collection of two or more posters by the same artist, whereby questions of artistic influence, development, and style might make fascinating further study by scholars whose foci are these artists.

DIGITIZING THE COLLECTION

In the fall of 2004, approximately 13 years after the posters were donated to the University of Illinois, the Slavic and East European Library took steps to begin digitizing the Winters Collection. At the outset, several points were researched and considered in discussions with various library units, such as the Preservation and Conservation Department; University Archives; and the Digital Services and Development Unit (DSD):

- An assessment of conservation/preservation needs for the posters;
- The need to construct a database for the collection using the typewritten finding aid;
- The conversion of the finding aid into electronic format by using the Encoding Archival Description (EAD);
- The need to decide upon an image database and delivery system;
- The selection of a metadata scheme;
- Copyright and reproduction permission issues.

At this time, a thorough assessment of the physical state of the posters was performed by the Preservation and Conservation Department of the Main Library, whereupon it was determined that only 11 of the posters had to undergo repairs. These repairs were also undertaken by the Preservation and Conservation Department.

When this project started, the available finding aid was in print form only (typed by hand around the time of the donation). No version of it in word-processed format could be located or found. Two efforts were pursued toward remedying this situation. First, a database in Microsoft Access was constructed, based on the content of the finding aid. Second, an electronic version of the finding aid was developed, using EAD (http://www.loc.gov/ead/), an open-source markup standard for making archival finding aids accessible in networked environments. (It should be noted that the Winters collection itself is housed in University Archives.) By early 2005, these two goals had been carried out, largely with the help of a graduate assistant.

The actual scanning of the posters would be carried out by DSD librarians and staff, and the Slavic Library would need to pay only for the cost of purchasing CD-ROMs on which to store the master images as preservation-quality TIFF files (a nominal price of about $100 for 10 CD-ROMs). When discussions took place regarding which software to use for keeping a database of the digital images and for delivering them, two systems were considered. One was CONTENTdm, a product developed originally at the University of Washington and used widely by libraries today. The other was the University of Michigan-owned DXLS XPAT tool, which has a robust search engine that is responsive to both

SGML- and XML-encoded texts.[5] The latter was considered because another project at the Slavic and East European Library, the hypertext archive *Early 19th-Century Russian Readership and Culture* (http://www.library.uiuc.edu/spx/rusread/) already uses it. However, most of the image collections at the University of Illinois are delivered via CONTENTdm; there are librarians and programmers at UIUC who have experience installing it, applying it to collections, and–as needed–troubleshooting it. As a result, the Slavic and East European Library decided to store and display the digital images through CONTENTdm.

With respect to a metadata standard to which to adhere for cataloging the digital images, the Visual Resources Association (VRA) Core Categories, version 3.0 (http://www.vraweb.org/vracore.htm), was chosen–although since this project was launched, the association has released a beta form of the VRA Core Categories, version 4.0. The main reason behind this decision lies in the characteristics that distinguish the categories that compose the VRA Core from those of other metadata schemes, such as Dublin Core: the VRA Core enables catalogers to create a metadata record for both the work of art (in the case of this project, for a poster) and for the digital image of that art work within the span of just one element set. The VRA Core Categories, version 3.0., were created for use in an array of database structures and image systems, so not surprisingly there has been no trouble implementing them in CONTENTdm.

Finally, because the Winters Collection consists of posters published in the twentieth century and because rights ownership for most of the posters is an unknown, copyright has emerged as an extraordinarily multifaceted, complex issue in this project. For many of the posters, there are layers of rights questions to navigate. For example, posters advertising a museum exhibit (of which there are many in the Winters Collection) can spawn these kinds of problems:

1. Who is considered the publisher if none is listed (and there is no name anywhere on the poster)–the museum?
2. Suppose that a poster has all of this information–the museum name, the name of the printing office that made copies of the poster, the name of the artist whose work is reproduced on the poster, and the name of the photographer who captured the image of a work–but no evidence of rights coverage or of the person or corporation who owns the rights;
3. The museum poster gives the name of the copyright owner but he is an artist who has died; and

4. The poster advertises an exhibit at a museum that no longer exists (and, once more, there is no publication or artist information).

The foregoing represent only some of the problems that are encountered in trying to digitize a visual resource collection of materials that are still covered under copyright law. The first step taken to address these copyright issues was to draft a general permissions letter (composed originally by a graduate student hired for the poster project, with input from Janice Pilch of the Slavic and East European Library, and written into final form by the Digital Content Creation Team at the University of Illinois Library). This letter was translated into Czech by Professor Frank Gladney, of the Department of Slavic and East European Languages and Literatures at the University of Illinois, and by Marie Kallista, a Library Technical Specialist and a native speaker of Czech. Thus, when this letter is sent out to prospective copyright holders, its text is in both English and Czech.

However, it rarely happens that a rights holder is located; either we are told that the organization to whom the letter was sent does not own the copyright to the poster, or we are referred to a possible rights holder, or we learn that, because of an organizational name change, it is simply unknown who owns the rights to the poster. In the meantime, the collection has not been made public (it is password-protected) and thus carries the following statement, displayed in the "Rights.Image" field: "The images on this site, from the Zdenka and Stanley B. Winters Czech and Slovak Poster Collection in the Slavic and East European Library at the University of Illinois at Urbana-Champaign, are provided to University of Illinois at Urbana-Champaign students, faculty and staff, and other researchers who visit this site, for research consultation and scholarly purposes only. Further distribution and/or any commercial use of the images from this site is not permitted."

At this writing approximately 100 posters remain to be scanned and catalogued. Meanwhile, related information has been assembled on the Winters Collection website (http://www.library.uiuc.edu/spx/winters/) to enrich the experience of the researcher. The site has six sections, as illustrated in Figure 1.

Three sections have already been discussed or touched on: Metadata, EAD, and Copyright Issues. Two others are worthy of further comment. The third heading on the page–OAI Resources–links to the UIUC Slavic Library's *OAI Resources* page. This page contains basic information on the Open Archives Initiative Protocol for Metadata Harvesting. The resources listed help to explain why it is important for digital projects to

FIGURE 1. Winters Collection Home Page

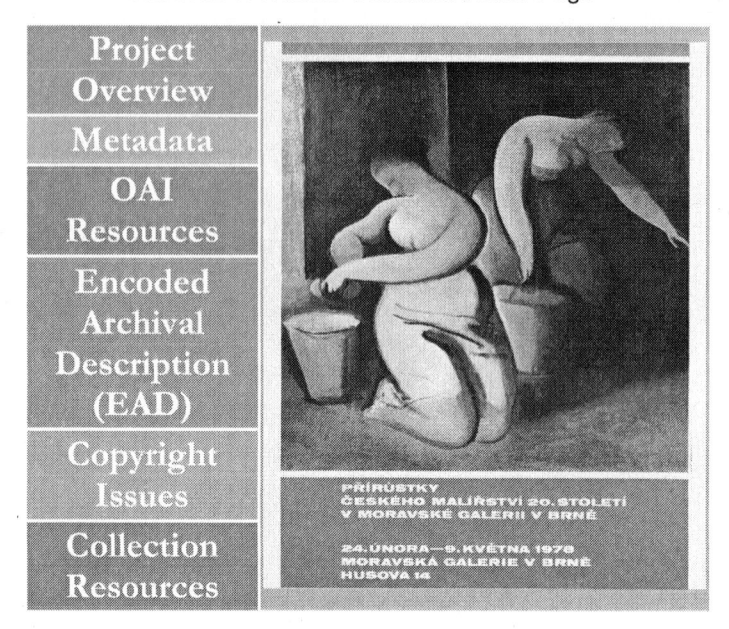

Used with permission.

serve as OAI Data Providers, and expose their metadata to OAI harvesters for data sharing via aggregated OAI Service providers like the University of Michigan's OAIster. It is the goal of the Slavic Library to establish all its digital initiatives as OAI Data Providers, as in the case of its *Inventory for Slavic, East European and Eurasian Digital Projects*, which contains 470 records for substantive digital projects all now searchable via OAIster.[6] There are also plans to do the same with Winters Collection metadata, so that Slavic researchers using these aggregated search services will discover the existence of these wonderful images and their accompanying resources much more easily.

Speaking of accompanying resources, the sixth heading on the website–Collection Resources–links to four groups of related material of interest to the researcher:

1. Books and articles;
2. Institutions featured in the posters;
3. Other Collections of Czech Posters;
4. Images of Czech posters.

Section 1 contains 43 citations to highly-relevant research on Czech graphic art. Section 2 contains links to the websites of 18 museums featured in the Winters Poster Collection. Section 3 contains links to information on three other substantial Czech poster collections. And Section 4 links to two online image collections of Czech posters. Finally, an additional resource prepared as digitization proceeded was a blog entitled *Postings on Posters: A Weblog about Digitizing the Winters Collection at UIUC*.[7] The blog is not presently linked from the main website because it was compiled in the period November 2005-June 2006 and is not currently maintained. But it contains much rich information, and there are plans, as resources permit, to activate the blog on a regular basis.

Thus, to researchers interested in art history, history, literature, music, and technology–all within the geographic and cultural regions that make up the Czech Republic and Slovakia–the Winters Collection constitutes an invaluable resource. Through diverse yet unique graphic design, including versatile applications of color, typeface, and text, these posters capture the rich, compelling narrative that is the history and culture of the former Czechoslovakia.

NOTES

1. The Winters poster collection is not the only special collection at the University of Illinois that highlights Czech and Slovak graphic culture. The Israel Perlstein collection of Czech and Slovak Book Design was acquired earlier by Senior Slavic Bibliographer Larry Miller from Perlstein, the well-known New York book dealer. The collection contains 750 signed limited bibliophile editions, many of which are beautiful examples of special bindings, or contain striking illustrations. Most were published in the former Czechoslovakia in the 1920s and 1930s. This collection, too, is a wonderful candidate for heightened access and preservation through digitization.

2. I wish to thank the following librarians for help and guidance with this project: Miranda Remnek, Roxanne Frey, Marie Kallista, Janice Pilch, and Helen Sullivan. Professor Frank Gladney of the Department of Slavic & East European Languages and Literatures provided expert translations as needed. Nuala Koetter, Amy Maroso, and the graduate assistants in Digital Services and Development proved invaluable assets when it came to learning CONTENTdm. In addition, I owe much to both Marc Gartler, who served as a graduate assistant on the project, and to Hana Jochcova, who translated (on a volunteer basis) most of the posters; both colleagues helped with the project in 2004-2005.

3. Books written and edited by Winters include the following: *Intellectual and Social Developments in the Habsburg Empire from Maria Theresa to World War 1: Essays Dedicated to Robert A. Kann*, ed. S. B. Winters and J. Held (Boulder: East

European Quarterly, 1975), including an essay by Winters entitled "Austroslavism, Panslavism, Russophilism in Czech Political Thought, 1870-1900"; *Czechs and Slovaks in the Twentieth Century = Tchèques et slovaques au vingtième siècle* (Tempe, AZ: Arizona State University, 1977); *The Jewish Question and Other Aspects of Modern Czechoslovakia* (Irvine, CA: Charles Schlacks, 1983); Robert A. Kann, *Dynasty, Politics and Culture: Selected Essays*, ed. S. B. Winters (Boulder: Social Science Monographs, 1991); and *T. G. Masaryk (1850-1937), vol. 1: Thinker and Politician*, ed. S. B. Winters (New York: St. Martin's Press, 1989).

4. Beyond these 488 posters are twenty extra, which are duplicates.

5. For more information on CONTENT.dm, see http://contentdm.com/. For XPAT see http://www.dlxs.org/products/xpat.html.

6. The UIUC Slavic Library's *OAI Resources* page can be found at http://www.library.uiuc.edu/spx/winters/OAI-page.htm. *OAIster* can be found at http://oaister.umdl.umich.edu/o/oaister/. The *Inventory for Slavic, East European and Eurasian Digital Projects* can be found at http://www.library.uiuc.edu/spx/inventory/index.htm.

7. The Winters Collection blog can be found at http://www.library.uiuc.edu/blog/cz_posters/.

doi:10.1300/J167v08n02_11

METADATA

Application of MARC21–Concise Format for Bibliographic Data in Bulgarian Libraries: The Case of the Central Library of the Bulgarian Academy of Sciences

Sabina Aneva

SUMMARY. The author discusses the application and use of MARC21–Concise Format for Bibliographic Data in Bulgarian libraries. The paper focuses on the adoption and development of the format in the Central Library of the Bulgarian Academy of Sciences, and the creation of tem-

---

Sabina Aneva is Deputy Director and Chief Systems Librarian, Central Library of the Bulgarian Academy of Sciences, 1, 15 Noemvri Street, 1040 Sofia, Bulgaria (E-mail: sabina@cl.bas.bg).

A related article by the author in Russian with a similar title is "Ispol'zovanie formata MARC21 v Tsentral'nom biblioteke Bolgarskoi akademii nauk" (Use of the MARC21 Format in the Central Library of the Bulgarian Academy of Sciences), *Bibliotechnyi forum Ukrainy* 2006, no. 3, 44-46.

[Haworth co-indexing entry note]: "Application of MARC21–Concise Format for Bibliographic Data in Bulgarian Libraries: The Case of the Central Library of the Bulgarian Academy of Sciences." Aneva, Sabina. Co-published simultaneously in *Slavic & East European Information Resources* (The Haworth Information Press, an imprint of The Haworth Press, Inc.) Vol. 8, No. 2/3, 2007, pp. 137-150; and: *Access to East European and Eurasian Culture: Publishing, Acquisitions, Digitization, Metadata* (ed: Miranda Remnek) The Haworth Information Press, an imprint of The Haworth Press, Inc., 2007, pp. 137-150. Single or multiple copies of this article are available for a fee from The Haworth Document Delivery Service [1-800-HAWORTH, 9:00 a.m. - 5:00 p.m. (EST). E-mail address: docdelivery@haworthpress.com].

Available online at http://seeir.haworthpress.com
© 2007 by The Haworth Press, Inc. All rights reserved.
doi:10.1300/J167v08n02_12

plates for bibliographic description that accommodate our traditional practices of bibliographic description and the specificities of Bulgarian publication activity. Explained in greater detail is the template for description of microfilms of medieval Slavic manuscripts. The author describes the field selections that have been made during the process of adopting of the MARC21 format, and the steps that have been taken to promote more widespread adoption of this metadata format in Bulgaria. doi:10.1300/J167v08n02_12 *[Article copies available for a fee from The Haworth Document Delivery Service: 1-800-HAWORTH. E-mail address: <docdelivery@haworthpress.com> Website: <http://www.HaworthPress.com> © 2007 by The Haworth Press, Inc. All rights reserved.]*

KEYWORDS. MARC21, Bulgaria, Bulgarian libraries, Central Library of the Bulgarian Academy of Sciences, medieval Slavic manuscripts, microfilms, cataloging, cataloguing

The very first efforts towards the normalization and standardization of data in Bulgaria date from 1932. In 1938 the Bulgarian Institute for Normalization (BIN) was organized. The first 112 Bulgarian norms were elaborated in 1938-1940.[1] In the 1990s the latest norms for bibliographic description of library materials were accepted by the Office of Standardization of the State Committee for Science and Technology (BNS [Bulgarian National Standard] 15419-82: Bibliographic Description of Books; BNS 15687-83: Bibliographic Description of Continuing Resourses, and so on). These are examples of the cataloging standards that were elaborated as an answer to traditional library needs, for the creation of hard copy cataloging cards, and their arrangement.

There have been many attempts at implementing modern information technologies in Bulgarian libraries during recent decades. The National Library "St. St. Cyril and Methodius"[2] is still maintaining its online catalogs on the platform of the UNESCO CDS/ISIS software package.[3] At the Library of Sofia University "St. Kliment Ohridski,"[4] ALEPH300 (ExLibris Ltd., Israel)[5] has been in use since the first half of the 1990s, and many other libraries in our country have developed their online catalogs based on domestic software products like e-Lib[6]; EL (AB–Electronic Library in Bulgarian),[7] and so on. The lack of Bulgarian, and generally-accepted international, standards for the bibliographic description of library materials in machine-readable form has led to various ambiguities and misunderstandings in the processes of cataloging contemporary library collections. Existing Bulgarian state standards for bibliographic description are old-fashioned, and satisfy only the needs of traditional, hard-copy libraries. They are not oriented towards making use of the vast opportunities offered by modern information technologies. In this situation, the idea of universal bibliographic control is not realizable at a national level, and at an international level is not possible at all. Discussions about which international format for description of library materials is best implemented nowadays in our library community have begun spontaneously. The format should provide standard bibliographic description of Bulgarian publishing production and give an opportunity for the exchange of bibliographic data with libraries abroad. Two major groups have been established in this regard: followers of the UNIMARC format, and those of MARC21.

Bulgarian libraries began the process of adopting MARC21 at the very peak of these theoretical debates. The implementation of contemporary library information systems both created and influenced the need for adopting international standards. As of April 2001, two university libraries–the Library of the New Bulgarian University[8] and the Library of the Technical University in Sofia[9]–have been using the Q-series LIS, the product of EOS International.[10] This system is distributed with the MARC21 format included, and librarians had to adopt the format without any prior experience or preliminary education.

Somewhat later, in January 1, 2003, the Central Library of the Bulgarian Academy of Sciences (BASCL)[11] began cataloging based on ALEPH500 LIS (ExLibris Ltd., Israel), MARC21 format,[12] and AACR2 (Anglo-American Cataloguing Rules 2).[13] This was the very first time that such a major Bulgarian library (the Central Library of the Bulgarian Academy of Sciences is one of the largest libraries in Bulgaria) had adopted an international library system based on international standards and norms not only for bibliographic data, but also for correspondences and accounting (EDI and so on).

We have accomplished a great deal of preliminary work for the future success of this activity by:

- Analyzing conditions and workflow under traditional circumstances;
- Changing the administrative structure of the library and preparing a new workflow;
- Setting up the integrated library system ALEPH 500, and investigating and adopting MARC21 Concise Format according to the specific needs of the Central Library and its 49 branch libraries;
- Developing a model for systems management;

- Preparing detailed manuals that are upgraded periodically and publishing them at the website of the Central Library[14];
- Providing continuing education for library staff.

The choice of MARC21–Concise Format for Bibliographic Data has imposed a need for developing several new templates according to AACR2, based on the traditional practices and functional structure of the BASCL and its branch libraries. These templates depend on:

- The software and additional services generated by it;
- The technological cycle of cataloging library materials;
- The type of library materials;
- The specific needs of users.

The main division of the templates for bibliographic data that was adopted in the BASCL is based on the type of library material:

- Monograph,
- Multi-volume work,
- Book Series,
- Cartographic Material,
- Music,
- Newspaper,
- Journal,
- Serials.

The template for bibliographic description of the *monograph* can be seen in Figure 1.

In the template in Figure 1, the first two fields are official and give us information about the database where the BIB record is saved and the corresponding system number. They are followed by the FMT field, which indicates the format of the library material–in this case BK (for books).

Next, two fields with fixed length are presented: Leader (LDR) and 008. The LDR field has 24 character positions (00-23). By default, in the LDR field the character position 05 (Record status) is filled with code *n* (New); 06 (Type of record) with code *a* (Language material); 07 (Bibliographic level) with code *m* (Monograph/item); 09 (Character coding scheme) with code *a* (UCS/Unicode); 18 (Descriptive cataloging form) with code *a* (AACR2). The tenth and eleventh positions are filled with code 2 that indicates the number of character positions used for indicators in a variable data field and the number of character posi-

FIGURE 1. Template for Bibliographic Description of the Monograph

DB		ASC01
SYSID		0
FMT		BK
LDR		^^^^^nam^a22^^^^^^a^4500
008		^^^^^^s2006^^^^bu^^^^^^r^^^^^000^0^bul^d
020	##	$a
040	##	$aBG-SoBAS
041	##	$a
044	##	$a
100	1#	$a $b $c $d $e $g $j $q
110	##	$a $b $c $d $e $f $k $n $t
111	##	$a $c $d $f $k $n $q $t
130	##	$a $f $k $p $t
240	1#	$a
245	0#	$a $b $c $n $p
246	##	$a $b $n $p
250	##	$a $b
260	##	$a $b $c
300	##	$a $b $c $e
500	##	$a
501	##	$a

FIGURE 1 (continued)

502	##	$a
504	##	$a
505	##	$g $r $t
546	##	$a $b
700	1#	$a $b $c $d $e $j $q
710	##	$a $b $c $d $e $f $k $n $t
711	##	$a $c $d $e $f $k $n $q $t
730	##	$a $f $k $p $t
740	##	$a $n $p

tions used for each subfield code in a variable data field. The positions 20-23 are numeric characters that indicate the structure of each entry in the Directory, and the value is 4500.

The first positions 00-05 of control field 008 are in *yymmdd* format (year, month, and day)–the date entered in the file. The field's next character positions are filled as follows: 06 (Type of date/Publication status) is filled by default with code *s* (Single known date/probable date); 07-10 (Date 1) with code *2006*; 15-17 (Place of publication, production, or execution) with code *bu* (Bulgaria)[15]; 23 (Form of item) with code *r* (Regular print reproduction); 29 (Conference publication) with code *0* (Not a conference publication); 30 (Festschrift) with code *0* (Not a festschrift); 31 (Index) with code *0* (No index); 33 (Literary form) with code *0* (Not fiction); 35-37 (Language) with code *bul* (Bulgarian)[16]; 39 (Cataloging source) with code *d* (Other).

After this, variable fields follow:

- Number and Code Fields (01X-04X): 020 (ISBN), 040 (Cataloging source)–filled with the code of the BASCL, 041 (Language code), 044 (Country of Publishing/Producing entity code);
- Main Entry Fields (1XX): 100 (Main Entry–Personal name), 110 (Main Entry–Corporate name), 111 (Main Entry–Meeting name), 130 (Main Entry–Uniform title);

- Title and Title-Related Fields (20X-24X): 240 (Uniform title), 245 (Title statement), 246 (Varying form of title);
- Edition, Imprint, etc. Fields (250-270): 250 (Edition statement), 260 (Publication, distribution, etc./imprint);
- Physical Description, etc. Fields (3XX): 300 (Physical description);
- Note Fields (Part 1: 50X-53X): 500 (General note), 501 (With note), 502 (Dissertation note), 504 (Bibliography, etc., note), 505 (formatted content note);
- Note Fields (Part 2: 53X-58X): 546 (Language note);
- Added Entry Fields (70X-75X): 700 (Added entry–Personal name), 710 (Added entry–Corporate name), 711 (Added entry–Meeting name), 730 (Uniform title), 740 (Uncontrolled related/analytical title).

Fields (6XX) are not presented in the template under consideration. This is because of the cataloging work flow at the BASCL: first, librarians from the department of Acquisition and Cataloging describe typical bibliographic fields, and then other specialists from the Classification and Indexing department add the subject fields. We have created a template that is used for this purpose only (Figure 2).

In the template in Figure 2, the following fields are presented:

- Classification and Call Number Fields (05X-08X): 080 (Universal Decimal Classification number);
- Subject Access Fields (6XX): 650 (Subject added entry–Topical term), 651 (Subject added entry–Geographic name), 653 (Index term–Uncontrolled), 655 (Index term–Genre/Form);
- The last field KDF is official, and its function is to format statistical and accounting data.

When we describe bibliographically a *multi-volume work* or *monographic series* we use analytical (hierarchical) links–UP and DOWN ANA LKR–between bibliographical records that give us options for monographic description of every single volume. There are also possibilities for the creation of parallel links (PAR LKR) in the following cases: two or more editions of a title; a title in different physical media, and a title in different languages. This type of link is in use for registering changes of title of periodicals. (See Figure 3).

When, moreover, we describe library materials on *DVD, CD, diskettes*, and so on, there are some special features:

FIGURE 2. Template for Classification and Indexing

080	##	$a $x
650	7#	$a $b $c $d $v $x $y $z $2
651	7#	$a $v $x $y $z $2
653	##	$a
655	7#	$a $b $c $v $x $y $z $2
KDF	##	$a

- FMT field: the format is changed from *BK* (Book), and so on, to *CF* (computer files);
- LDR field: character position 06 (Type of record) is filled by default with code *m* (Computer file);
- Edition, Imprint, etc. (Fields 250-270): here we use Field 256 (Computer file characteristics);
- Note Fields (Part 2: 53X-58X): here we use Field 538 (System details note).

The templates for bibliographic records of *Cartographic Material* and *Music* are based on the templates for books, but with some special features:

- FMT: the format is changed from *BK* (Book) to *MP* (Maps), *MU* (Scores);
- LDR: character position 06 (Type of record) is filled with code *c* (Notated music), *d* (Manuscript notated music), *e* (Cartographic material), or *f* (Manuscript cartographic material);
- 008: when the described library materials are maps, we fill the following character positions: 18-21 (Relief), 25 (Type of cartographic material); when it is a set of scores: 18-19 (Form of composition), 20 (Format of music), 21 (Music parts), 22 (Target audience);
- Number and Code Fields (01X-04X), which are variable fields: we use 034 (Coded cartographic mathematical data);
- Edition, Imprint, etc. Fields 250-270 (also variable fields): we use 255 (Cartographic mathematical data). This data may also be coded in field 034.

The template for bibliographic description of *microfilms of medieval manuscripts* is of special interest for our library. It is based on the format for description of manuscripts created by Prof. David Birnbaum of the University in Pittsburgh, USA[17]; Prof. Anissava Miltenova of the Institute of Literature of the Bulgarian Academy of Sciences, Bulgaria; and Prof. Andrei Boyadzhiev of Sofia University, Bulgaria. It represents metadata in XML (Extensible Markup Language). Our template is developed with the idea that it will give us options for exporting and importing data from one format to another. The template appears in Figure 4.

The template in Figure 4 includes the following fields:

- FMT: the format used is *BK* (Books).
- LDR: character position 05 (Record status) is filled by default with code *n* (New); and 06 (Type of record) with code *t* (Manuscript language material). The other character positions in the LDR field

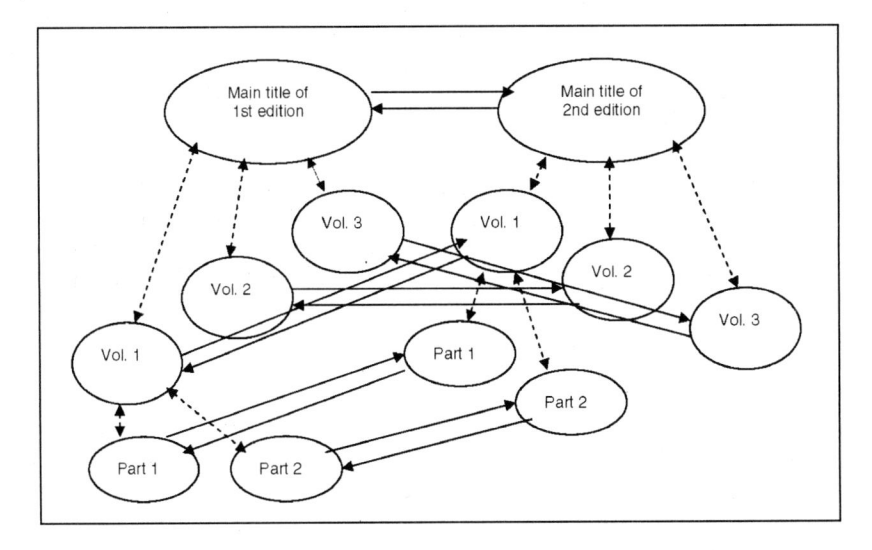

FIGURE 3. Parallel and Analytical Links

Legend:

Analytical link ◀------▶

Parallel link ───────▶

FIGURE 4. Template for Description of Microfilms of Medieval Manuscripts

DB		ASC01
SYSID		0
FMT		BK
LDR		^^^^^ntm^a22^^^^^^a^4500
007		hd^afb^^^baca
008		^^^^^^nuuuuuuuubu^^^^^^a^^^^^|00^0^chu^d
040	##	$aBG-SoBAS
041	0#	$achu
044	##	$a
130	0#	$a $f $k $p $t
242	1#	$a $h[microfilm]$b $c $n $p $yeng
245	1#	$a $h[microfilm]$b $c $n $p $f
246	##	$a $b $n $p
300	##	$a $cmm.$b $e
300	##	$aff.$cmm.$b $e
500	##	$aMaterial Description :
500	##	$aCondition :
546	##	$aLanguage :$b Script :
546	##	$a
520	2#	$a $b
500	##	$aNotes Description :

FIGURE 4 (continued)

535	1#	$3 $a $b $c $d $g
541	1#	$3 $a $d
581	##	$a
533	##	$aMicrofilm$b $c $d $e1 microfilm reel : positive ; 35 mm.$n
700	##	$a $b $c $d $etranscriber$j $q
710	2#	$a $b $c $d $eowner$f $k $n $t

for this template are filled with the same values as noted above in the description of our monographic template.
- However, unlike the monographic template, which moves directly from LDR to 008, in this template we have entered the field 007. It is filled in character position 00 (Category of material) with code *h* (Microform); 01 (Specific material designation) with code *d* (Microfilm reel); 03 (Positive/negative aspect) with code *a* (Positive); 04 (Dimensions) with code *f* (35 mm); 05 (Reduction ratio range) with code *b* (Normal reduction); 09 (Color) with code *b* (Black-and-white (or monochrome); 10 (Emulsion on film) with code *a* (Silver halide); 11 (Generation) with code *c* (Service copy); 12 (Base of film) with code *a* (Safety base, undetermined). Use of these codes provides a rich overview of the film at hand.
- Then we move to Field 008. Character position 06 (Type of date/ Publication status) is filled by default with code *n* (Dates unknown); position 07-10 (Date 1) and 11-14 (Date 2) with code *u* (Date element is totally or partially unknown); 15-17 (Place of publication, production, or execution) with code *bu* (Bulgaria); 23 (Form of item) with code *a* (Microfilm); 29 (Conference publication) with code *0* (Not a conference publication); 30 (Festschrift) with code *0* (Not a festschrift); 31 (Index) with code *0* (No index); 33 (Literary form) with code *0* (Not fiction/not further specified); 35-37 (Language) with *chu* (Church Slavic); 39 (Cataloging source) with code *d* (Other).

Hereinafter the variable fields for the description of manuscripts on film that are different from the template for monographs are listed:

- Number and Code Fields (01X-04X): the missing field is 020 (ISBN);
- Main Entry Fields (1XX): the missing fields are 100 (Main entry–Personal name), 110 (Main entry–Corporate name), 111 (Main entry–Meeting name). Only the field 130 (Main entry–Uniform title) is used;
- Title and Title-Related Fields (20X-24X): in use is field 242 (Translation of title by cataloging agency); missing is field 240 (Uniform title);
- Note Fields (Part 1: 50X-53X): fields 501 (With note), 502 (Designation note), 504 (Bibliography, etc. note), 505 (Formatted contents note) are missing. Fields that are not missing: 500 (General note) with defined front matter because this too should be exported/imported to/from XML format, 520 (Summary, etc.), 533 (Reproduction note), 535 (Location of originals/duplicates note);
- Note Fields (Part 2: 53X-58X): fields in use are 546 (Language note) with defined front matter because this too should be exported/imported to/from XML format, 541 (Immediate source of acquisition note), 581 (Publications about described materials note). This last field is an extremely valuable means of enriching the content of our records;
- Added Entry Fields (70X-75X): fields in use are 700 (Added entry–Personal name), 710 (Added entry–Corporate name).

Lastly, not included in detail here are the templates for bibliographic description of *newspapers* and *journals*, and for *serials*, which follow the same kinds of codings, with obvious exceptions to indicate publications in progress, when necessary.

As indicated, the templates for bibliographic data of the Central Library of the Bulgarian Academy of Sciences are now created according to MARC21–Concise Format for Bibliographic Data and AACR2, and are also compatible with the traditional practices of our own library cataloging. The bibliographic records are very detailed, and pay special attention to analytical descriptions. The subject indexing is also very detailed; the fields are filled with word equivalents to a Universal Decimal Classification number while following local systematic cataloging traditions. At the same time, our BIB records are totally compatible with international standards. As a result, and thanks to the Z39.50 search-

and-retrieve protocol, we are exchanging bibliographic data with many libraries in Bulgaria as well as abroad. In addition, and very significantly, with the implementation of the next version of ALEPH500 (version 16), we are planning to set up an X-Server that will give us an opportunity to export bibliographic metadata in MARC XML format. And it should also be noted that the Central Library of the Bulgarian Academy of Sciences has prepared templates for descriptions that are created according to MARC21–Concise Format for Authority Data,[18] and MARC21–Concise Format for Holding Data.[19]

Colleagues from the Library of Congress who have advised us have determined our BIB records to be extremely good and highly professional. This is the reason why our library has been nominated as a MARC21 Knowledge Center for Bulgaria. This means that we are entitled to act as consultants, give advice, and share expertise with local libraries that already have, or may develop, a professional interest in MARC21. In 2003 we organized a MARC21 e-Club. Its members are employees of the Central Library of the Bulgarian Academy of Sciences, and the libraries of the New Bulgarian University, Technical University in Sofia, and the American University–Bulgaria. Many MARC21-related questions and problems are discussed. The MARC21 e-Club has its own website[20] and mailing list: BGMARC@cl.bas.bg.

Finally, an ambitious program for the translation of basic MARC21 documentation has been developed. The very first step is a translation of *Understanding MARC Bibliographic: Machine Readable Cataloging*.[21] Also expected is a publication that will share the expertise accumulated during different aspects of the adoption and application of MARC21 format for bibliographic metadata in the Central Library of the Bulgarian Academy of Sciences and its 49 branch libraries.

NOTES

1. Bulgarian Institute for Standardization, *Facts and Figures*, http://www.bds-bg.org/site/EN/about_us.html (accessed October 23, 2006).

2. National Library "St. St. Cyril and Methodius," http://www.nationallibrary.bg/ (accessed July 11, 2006).

3. Communication and Information: UNESCO–CI, *CDS/ISIS Database Software: UNESCO–CI,* http://portal.unesco.org/ci/en/ev.php-URL_ID=2071&URL_DO=DO_TOPIC&URL_SECTION = 201.html (accessed July 11, 2006).

4. Library of Sofia University "St. Kliment Ohridski," http://www.libsu.uni-sofia.bg/ (accessed July 11, 2006).

5. ExLibris, *Aleph–Overview,* http://www.exlibrisgroup.com/aleph.htm (accessed July 11, 2006).
6. SoftLib Ltd., http://www.softlib.primasoft.bg/ (accessed July 11, 2006).
7. PC-TM Ltd., http://www.pc-tm.com/pctmbg/default.htm (accessed July 11, 2006).
8. Nov Bulgarski Universitet, *Bibliotechen kompleks* (Library Complex), http://www.nbu.bg/index.php?l=27 (accessed July 11, 2006).
9. Tekhnicheski Universitet-Sofiia, Bibliotechno Informatsion en Kompleks, *Elektronen Katalog* (Electronic Catalog), http://libserve.tu-sofia.bg/WebOPAC/index.asp (accessed July 11, 2006).
10. EOS International: Delivery Library Automation, Content, and Knowledge Management Solution, http://www.eosintl.com/ (accessed July 11, 2006).
11. Central Library of the Bulgarian Academy of Sciences, http://www.cl.bas.bg/ (accessed July 11, 2006).
12. The Library of Congress, *MARC21 Concise Format for Bibliographic Data,* http://www.loc.gov/marc/bibliographic/ecbdhome.html (accessed July 13, 2006).
13. Anglo-American Cataloguing Rules 2, http://www.aacr2.org/ (accessed July 11, 2006).
14. Central Library of Bulgarian Academy of Sciences, *Inside,* http://www.cl.bas.bg/inside/ (accessed July 12, 2006).
15. The code recorded in 008/15-17 is used in conjunction with field 044 (Country of Publishing/Producing entity code) when more than one code is appropriate to an item.
16. The code recorded in 008/35-37 is used in conjunction with field 041 (Language code).
17. David J. Birnbaum [Home Page], http://clover.slavic.pitt.edu/~djb/ (accessed July 13, 2006).
18. The Library of Congress, *MARC21 Concise Format for Authority Data,* http://www.loc.gov/marc/authority/ecadhome.html (accessed July 13, 2006).
19. The Library of Congress, *MARC21 Concise Format for Holdings Data,* http://www.loc.gov/marc/holdings/echdhome.html (accessed July 13, 2006).
20. Club MARC21, http://cl.bas.bg/marc21/ (accessed July 13, 2006).
21. Betty Furrie, *Understanding MARC Bibliographic: Machine Readable Cataloging* (2003) http://www.loc.gov/marc/umb/ (accessed July 13, 2006).

doi:10.1300/J167v08n02_12

The Librarian's Role in Promoting Digital Scholarship: Development and Metadata Issues

Eileen Llona

SUMMARY. Digital technology is being used increasingly in humanities and social science scholarship. Librarians offer a unique set of skills that can assist in providing access to digitally created knowledge, and its preservation. This essay offers a basic overview of the steps involved in digital scholarship, and how librarians can participate in its development. Also presented is a brief introduction to technological issues with which librarians should be familiar, including new metadata challenges. doi:10.1300/J167v08n02_13 *[Article copies available for a fee from The Haworth Document Delivery Service: 1-800-HAWORTH. E-mail address: <docdelivery@haworthpress.com> Website: <http://www.HaworthPress.com> © 2007 by The Haworth Press, Inc. All rights reserved.]*

KEYWORDS. Digital scholarship, metadata, humanities, social sciences, technology analog

---

Eileen Llona, MLIS, is International Studies Computer Services Librarian, Digital Initiatives, University of Washington Libraries, Box 352900, Seattle WA 98195 USA (E-mail: ellona@u.washington.edu).

[Haworth co-indexing entry note]: "The Librarian's Role in Promoting Digital Scholarship: Development and Metadata Issues." Llona, Eileen. Co-published simultaneously in *Slavic & East European Information Resources* (The Haworth Information Press, an imprint of The Haworth Press, Inc.) Vol. 8, No. 2/3, 2007, pp. 151-163; and: *Access to East European and Eurasian Culture: Publishing, Acquisitions, Digitization, Metadata* (ed: Miranda Remnek) The Haworth Information Press, an imprint of The Haworth Press, Inc., 2007, pp. 151-163. Single or multiple copies of this article are available for a fee from The Haworth Document Delivery Service [1-800-HAWORTH, 9:00 a.m. - 5:00 p.m. (EST). E-mail address: docdelivery@haworthpress.com].

Available online at http://seeir.haworthpress.com
© 2007 by The Haworth Press, Inc. All rights reserved.
doi:10.1300/J167v08n02_13

BACKGROUND

Scholarship in both the sciences and arts/humanities has begun to make increasing use of technology to analyze information, as well as to create new knowledge. Digital hardware and software are employed not only to collect information (such as field recordings or other field-based data collection), but also for the analysis of existing data (as in the use of image processing software for image analysis), and its dissemination. The science disciplines have made heavy use of technology for collecting and interpreting data for years, and more recently, humanities and social science scholars have been incorporating technology into their analysis of cultural resources. Interdisciplinary research is growing in large part due to advances in technological infrastructure, and digital technologies offer a large potential for transforming research and teaching. Indeed, this potential is being realized through many projects in the arts and humanities. Examples include projects from long-standing digitally supported programs such as the University of Virginia's Institute for Advanced Technology in the Humanities[1] and the California Digital Library eScholarship[2] program. While these programs, and the projects that have resulted from them, exemplify the promise that digital technologies have brought to the scholar and the student in both research and teaching/learning situations, the learning curve required to use technology in new and innovative ways has hampered its widespread adoption, especially in the arts and humanities. It is fairly simple to create electronic documents using a word processor; it takes time, energy and interest to use more complex software tools to transform the ways in which analysis, interpretation, and presentation of information are performed. This burden can be lightened through collaboration, both within one's own field and beyond, and should include partnerships with librarians and technologists.

Much has been written about the application and impact of digital technology in humanities, arts, and social science research and teaching (a sampling of which is included in the attached bibliography). The goal of this article is to introduce the concept of digital scholarship to Slavic librarians and scholars who may not yet be involved in these processes, and to provide a broad overview of the more obvious issues that need to be considered when supporting digital scholarship. I especially encourage Slavic studies librarians to talk with faculty about digital projects they are involved with, and be willing to "think outside the box" of traditional librarianship in order to promote innovative ways of accessing and using digital resources. Following is a brief definition of digital scholarship, a description of why librarians need to pay attention to it, and an overview of technical issues commonly encountered in working with digital scholarship.

WHAT IS DIGITAL SCHOLARSHIP?

Digital scholarship refers to research products, results, and tools that are either born digital, or have been converted from analog to digital format. Often this type of scholarship stems from the discovery of new knowledge as a result of using technology to gather, analyze, or publish data, usually for the purpose of research or teaching. Digital scholarship can refer to electronic publications, such as e-books or electronic journals, but often encompasses a wide variety of file formats and media types, such as audio, video, and images. Activities may range from simply digitizing existing analog primary sources to using text analysis technologies, geographic information systems, and audio manipulation software to analyze data and create "published" work that incorporates these various data types and file formats. These newer forms of publication often provide access to raw data in new and interesting ways, such as the use of interactive maps, accompanying video/audio files, and other features that add contextual value to the content. Examples include websites, desktop digital objects, self-authored software, and electronic archives. Scholarship that is produced or augmented digitally may consist in experimenting with new methodologies of obtaining information and performing research and analysis; creating electronic archives that can be developed over time; providing interactivity and capturing user interactions as part of data collection and scholarship; providing multiple media types for "experiencing" the data for research and teaching; and creating local, non-published projects that may have valuable content, but are not available through the Internet or other widely available means.[3]

BARRIERS AND CONSTRAINTS TO THE MANAGEMENT OF DIGITAL SCHOLARSHIP

Despite the growth of technology, and the innovative ways that scholars employ it, the widespread use of digital technologies for producing scholarship is hampered for a variety of reasons. In many cases, researchers will produce innovative websites that utilize a variety of technologies, often hosting these sites through departmental accounts or even from their home computers. These sites, or digital projects, may be used in teaching, or may be used by individual scholars or shared among colleagues to enhance teaching and research on a particular topic. But when the scholars retire, or leave the institution, support for their handcrafted resources may or may not be continued. It is often at these times that the library is approached to "take ownership" of these resources in terms of collection or preservation. Lack of infrastructure from the beginning makes the lifetime of these kinds of projects questionable, even if the content value is high.

Confusion about copyright issues is another constraint on producing, and preserving, digital scholarship. One of the important roles that librarians can serve is to educate scholars about their rights and options for copyrighting their material. Understanding the copyright constraints associated with commercial publishers (such as for e-publications) and alternatives (such as the flexible copyright options offered by Creative Commons)[4] can help researchers and librarians make digital scholarship available along with appropriate copyright protection. Licensing components of content from the digital resource is often an issue, and faculty should work closely with their institution's technology transfer office, as well as copyright experts in the library or other administrative offices.

The constant change in technology standards is another reason why scholars are unwilling to pursue digital scholarship, and institutions are unwilling to provide the necessary infrastructure to support this new form of scholarship. Concerns about the long-term preservation of file formats and programs will often cause archiving organizations to balk at accepting digital projects. Who will be responsible for migrating formats? Are there accepted file formats that are likely to be usable in the future? Who will provide the metadata, and how? Questions such as these don't have solid answers yet, though the digital library world is actively looking at these issues; and answers, or at least best practices, are starting to appear.

Finally, a significant constraint to good management of digital scholarship is metadata. Scholars may be able to produce wonderful resources using creative combinations of technology to make a point, either for research or teaching, but sometimes the description of these projects, and how the pieces fit together, proves to be a huge challenge. Do we record specific software components and requirements? Do we need to describe how the audio file "fits" with the text in a document? What exactly do we inventory? Again, this is a new avenue of metadata development that has no clear answers at this point. But it is important to be aware of the problems. As librarians and researchers, we have an important role to play in applying our traditional training and interest in cataloging and content description to this new form of scholarship.

WHY SHOULD LIBRARIANS CARE?

Librarians in all disciplines–and also Slavic studies–are increasingly involved in digital scholarship. Researchers are coming to libraries not only for assistance in preserving the scholarship they create, but also for advice on information architecture. As librarians we play an important role in selecting and preserving scholarship, but we also have much knowledge to contribute to scholars as they create new forms of scholarly output. Our expertise in metadata, content description, and search and access methods is needed to ensure that new forms of scholarship survive into the future.

The challenge as regards describing complex digital objects is considerable; we must not only describe the whole, we must understand the components, and the technologies required to access them. We must understand storage requirements, software platforms, file formats, and metadata standards. The role of the librarian has quickly assumed an aspect of digital stewardship. Our traditional activities–cataloging, acquisition, bibliographic instruction, and preservation–will continue with new forms of scholarship, but the tools we use and the ways we will be required to view scholarship, catalog it, and make it available, will continue to change. Many examples of digital scholarship exist that cannot be printed out and saved on paper for preservation purposes. We must use specialized software to open it; we must have access to large amounts of storage space, and ways to describe components that accommodate hierarchical relationships.

The downtrend in academic publishing has concerned librarians who acquire traditional, print monographic publications. The cost of print publications has forced many academic publishers to close, or has caused the cost to be shifted to authors. Academic publishers often can't or won't publish monographs due to the high publication costs. Digital scholarship is allowing younger researchers to create and publish their own works. As an example of current trends in digital scholarship, Rice University Press now focuses exclusively on digital publications, allowing authors to include multimedia, and offering a method of peer review of these digitally-produced scholarly works.[5]

If the trend toward digital scholarship continues, as seems likely, librarians will need to understand how these publications are put together, and the requirements for preservation and access. The changing nature of information requires us to be more active collaborators in digital scholarship; indeed, this collaboration is often requested by scholars, in terms of having the librarian provide guidance on format and metadata standards, and provide instruction in the use of such standards, and how to search, access, and cite existing digital projects.

ENABLING DIGITAL SCHOLARSHIP: THE LIBRARIAN'S ROLE

Work in digital library projects–including Slavic projects–involves being familiar with all aspects of the enterprise, from funding to preservation. We don't have to be experts, but we should at least be aware of what it takes to produce digital scholarship. Subject librarians who are already performing acquisitions, selection, and cataloging functions are also being asked to address the acquisition of new content in electronic form, either from vendors or from their constituent faculty. This may be in the form of collaborating in the creation of content through digitization, or obtaining already authored digital material. Grant writing, selection, cataloging, and preservation are functions that will continue to be needed in the realm of digital scholarship. However, what is changing is the extent to which we participate in each of these activities. Basically, librarians need to understand the new forms that scholarship takes, and support these new forms by providing access and preservation mechanisms.

Collaboration between librarians and scholars already exists in the form of partnerships between scholars and librarians to digitize existing analog resources. At a minimum, librarians should be familiar with digitization standards for various analog formats (such as text and images). Librarians are well-positioned to establish partnerships between library infrastructure (technical services as well as staffing), academic departments, and publishers to ensure that standards are understood and utilized where appropriate. In order to foster these partnerships, librarians might consider involvement in grant writing, some degree of information architecture, metadata consulting and/or creation, and data storage decisions.

Funding

Funding opportunities for digital projects in the humanities are often hard to find, though more institutions are offering grants in this realm. For example, the National Endowment for the Humanities recently (Summer 2006) announced a new Digital Humanities Initiative, encouraging the submission of projects that use technology. "NEH is interested in fostering the growth of digital humanities and lending support to a wide variety of projects, including those that deploy digital technologies and methods to enhance our understanding of a topic or issue; those that study the impact of digital technology on the humanities– exploring the ways in which it changes how we read, write, think, and learn; and those that digitize important materials thereby increasing the public's ability to search and access humanities information."[6] Librarians can and should be involved in many of these grant opportunities, since at some point many of the resources that are created from these grants will probably be deposited at the library for access, archiving, and preservation.

Other organizations that provide funding for digital scholarship, including library collaboration, include the Institute of Museum and Library Services (IMLS)[7], the Andrew Mellon Foundation,[8] and the U.S. Department of Education's Technological Innovation and Cooperation for Foreign Information Access program.[9] In many cases, funding agencies are looking for collaboration between institutions and divisions, and will often favor interdisciplinary collaboration that includes libraries, since this shows an intent to use standards and provide some means of preservation of any resulting resources.

File Formats

Supporting digital scholarship requires being familiar with the range of software and hardware types that may be encountered for any given project. This does not mean that librarians need extensive technical knowledge; however, being able to understand the basics of file formats and metadata standards will be an advantage in working with these projects. Many projects will incorporate a variety of media, including text, still images, moving images, and audio. There are many options for these types of digital objects, but best practices and standards are emerging that provide some guidance regarding the reliability of certain formats for interchange and preservation. Below is a brief overview of common media types and file formats that will likely be encountered in

Slavic studies projects. There are several published guidelines that offer discussions of media types and preferred file formats for preservation purposes, such as the NINCH Guide,[10] Arts and Humanities Data Service,[11] technical guidelines from the National Archives and Records Administration,[12] and The Florida Center for Library Automation.[13] The reader is encouraged to review these sources for more detailed information on digital file formats.

Text Files

The most basic format for text is plain text files, usually with an extension of .txt. These files do not include any formatting code or markup. Plain text files may be encoded to indicate the character set used in the file. ASCII is the most widely used encoding, but it does not handle most of the characters used in non-English languages. Therefore, other encodings must be incorporated into the file if non-English language is represented. There are many language-specific encodings (Cyrillic has several, including ISO-8859-5, Windows-1251, and KOI8-R), though the transferability and preservation potential of these encodings is not great. Unicode is an encoding that includes the scripts and diacritics of most languages of the world, and has come to be the most suitable for preservation. Thus, when looking at files or talking about text formats, look for and encourage Unicode encoding (either 8-bit or 16-bit).

Text may also come in formatted files, such as word processed files (.doc, .rtf, .wpd) or postscript files (.pdf, .ps). All of these binary formats use proprietary commercial software, and because of this, the ability to ensure migration and readability into the future is questionable. It is thus advisable to encourage digital scholars to use plain text formats with Unicode encoding for text files whenever possible.

Images

Still images are perhaps most ubiquitous in digital scholarship (aside from electronic text). Digital images can be in uncompressed formats (.tiff, .png) or compressed (.jpg, .gif, compressed .tiff). Most digitization guidelines recommend that the Tagged Image File Format (TIFF) in uncompressed form is the preferred format for digital images–since the file with the most resolution and least/no compression will provide the best preservation copy. Compressed file formats are often used for web presentation, but generally are not the preferred format for archival purposes. If used, the compression should be lossless (i.e., achieved by means of an algorithm that saves all data), since the file is then more suitable for migration and preservation. A lossy compression (when data is lost, as in .jpg) is clearly unsuitable for archiving. Digital scholars should be encouraged to include .tiff or .png versions of images used in their projects.

Video

Moving images (video) also come in a variety of file formats, most of which are compressed. Digital video separates the video from the audio, so different compression schemes can be applied for each media type. In general, the MPEG standard is most recommended for preservation due to its non-proprietary format (i.e., many software brands can read mpeg files), while formats such as Quicktime (.mov, .qt) and Microsoft's Audio/Video Interleaved (.avi) formats require proprietary software, and are not recommended for digital projects that should be saved into the future.

Audio

As with image formats, audio files come in uncompressed and compressed formats. Again, uncompressed formats are most suitable for preservation and migration; these include Microsoft's WAVE PCM encodings (.wav), and Apple's Audio Interchange File Format (.aiff). Due to the uncompressed nature of these files, however, file sizes will be much larger than compressed files, which are more widely distributed. The MPEG Layer 3 (.mp3) format is the most popular, with Real Audio and Ogg also prevalent. Because the compression standards are still in flux, none of them are appropriate for preservation purposes, though digital projects will likely use them due to their smaller file sizes.

Metadata Standards

Metadata is data about data; it represents the cataloging, or indexing, information for digital objects. Librarians can apply similar theories and practices to the addition of metadata to digital projects, though with the growth of electronic material, it is becoming more difficult for libraries to be the only source of metadata. As with catalog data, metadata allows for the retrieval of digital objects through systems similar to online library catalogs. Metadata can even be mapped to existing catalogs using crosswalks between metadata and the MARC bibliographic standard. Metadata can describe the content of a digital object (descriptive or bibliographic-like metadata), the format of the digital file (technical metadata), or its rights management (administrative metadata).

The current best practice for documenting metadata is to use XML (Extensible Markup Language). XML provides tagged elements, which are the equivalent of field names or labels (such as title, author, etc.). Schemas are definitions and rules about how metadata should be structured for a particular subject or use. Dublin Core (DC)[14] is the simplest schema, and it is considered the lowest common denominator for describing digital objects, including web pages, image files, and text files. This schema is recommended for applying a minimal set of metadata to an object or set of digital objects. Since there are only nine recommended elements, it is the easiest to use, and there are many websites that will generate DC by filling out a form.[15]

The most commonly used XML schemas in the library field are the Metadata Object Description Standard (MODS), and Encoded Archival Description (EAD). Detailed information on these schemas can be found from the Library of Congress.[16] The Metadata Encoding and Transmission Standard (METS) is a complex schema that can be used as a "wrapper" for other metadata, including descriptive, technical, and administrative schemas. It is useful in describing complex digital objects (for example, a digitized book that might have PDFs and TIFFs can all be described using one METS file). Other descriptive metadata schemas that may be appropriate for Slavic materials include VRA Core (for cultural objects) and CDWA-Lite.

Most digital objects can be described by using metadata as external files (similar in concept to the idea of a bibliographic record describing a monograph). However, some metadata schemas such as the Text Encoding Initiative (TEI)[17] embed tags into textual content, for the purposes of analysis and extraction. In Slavic studies, many digital projects are based on textual materials, and TEI may be encountered frequently. The Digital Library Foundation has produced a set of recommendations and guidelines for use of TEI in libraries.[18] The reader is encouraged to become familiar with this schema, since one of its strengths is to allow the analysis of textual material, which can also be leveraged to enhance description of digital content for access purposes.

Image formats, such as TIFF and Photoshop formats (.psd), can also embed metadata in the headers of the files. This type of metadata can be extracted using programmatic methods and tools such as

ImageMagick[19] or JHOVE.[20] The technical details of this extraction are beyond the scope of this article; however, the option is mentioned to promote collaboration among colleagues, including subject and technical specialists.

How Do We Preserve and Provide Access to Digital Scholarship?

The storage of digital projects, and provision of search mechanisms, present several issues. Large amounts of storage are usually needed, and specialized software is often used to access and display digital scholarship. Issues of software migration and accessibility are complex, and easy answers are not widely available. Understanding file formats and software compatibility, and using standards and best practices as often as possible, are currently the best methods for ensuring access to these projects in the future.

Institutional repositories are collections of digital material produced by an institution, usually a university or an academic discipline. The infrastructure of an institutional repository includes software (such as DSpace or Fedora), as well as a commitment to provide ongoing data storage hardware and staffing. Several universities are committing to the idea of supporting an institutional repository by providing IR software and staffing, while some disciplinary-specific repositories have been developed and are maintained by professional organizations.[21] Several models for storing and providing access to digital scholarship are being developed, but as yet no single solution has become clear. At a minimum, institutions need to form a commitment to the preservation of digital scholarship, and by understanding the issues involved in supporting this scholarship, librarians can play an important role in decisions that assist this commitment.

CONCLUSIONS

Technology is enabling change to occur at a rapid pace, and this change touches much of society. As stewards of information, librarians have an obvious role to play in ensuring appropriate use and preservation of digital materials that are created due to advances in technology. The new knowledge that technology allows us to discover should not be wasted simply because we are unwilling to adapt to new ways of describing content. By becoming comfortable with the basics of technology, managing the pace of change, and looking at new ways to apply traditional and valuable theories, librarians can actively participate in the next generation of scholarship.

NOTES

1. Institute for Advanced Technology in the Humanities, http://www.iath.virqinia.edu/ (accessed July 31, 2006).
2. California Digital Library eScholarship program, http://www.escholarship.cdlib.org/ (accessed July 31, 2006).
3. Abby Smith, *New-model Scholarship: How Will It Survive?* (Washington: Council on Library and Information Resources, March 2003).
4. Creative Commons, http://creativecommons.org/ (accessed November 3, 2006).
5. Rice University Press, http://ricepress.rice.edu/news.html (accessed November 3, 2006).
6. National Endowment for the Humanities, http://www.neh.gov/grants/digitalhumanities.html (accessed July 29, 2006).
7. Institute of Museum and Library Services (IMLS), http://www.imls.gov/ (accessed August 3, 2006).
8. Andrew W. Mellon Foundation, http://www.mellon.org/ (accessed August 3, 2006).
9. Technological Innovation and Cooperation for Foreign Information Access, http://www.ed.gov/programs/iegpsticfia/index.html (accessed August 3, 2006).
10. National Initiative for a Networked Cultural Heritage, *"NINCH Guide to Good Practice in the Digital Representation and Management of Cultural Heritage Materials,"* http://www.nyu.edu/its/humanities/ninchguide/ (accessed August 3, 2006).
11. Arts and Humanities Data Service, "AHDS Repository Policies and Procedures," http://www.ahds.ac.uk/preservation/ahds-preservation-documents.htm (accessed July 31, 2006).
12. U.S. National Archives and Records Administration (NARA), "Technical Guidelines for Digitizing Archival Materials for Electronic Access: Creation of Production Master Files–Raster Images," http://www.archives.gov/research/arc/digitizing-archival-materials.pdf (accessed August 3, 2006).
13. The Florida Center for Library Automation, http://www.fcla.edu/ (accessed July 31, 2006).
14. Dublin Core Metadata Initiative (DCMI), http://www.dublincore.org/ (accessed August 2, 2006).
15. For example, see "DescribeThis: Metadata Services and Tools," http://www.describethis.com/ (accessed August 2, 2006).
16. The Library of Congress, *Standards*, http://www.loc.gov/standards/ (accessed August 2, 2006).
17. *TEI: Yesterday's Information Tomorrow*, http://www.tei-c.org (accessed August 2, 2006).
18. *TEI in Libraries*, http://www.diglib.org/standards/tei.htm (accessed August 2, 2006).
19. *ImageMagick: Convert, Edit and Compose Images*, http://www.imagemagick.org/script/index.php (accessed August 2, 2006).
20. *JHOVE–JSTOR: Harvard Object Validation Environment*, http://hul.harvard.edu/jhove/ (accessed August 2, 2006).
21. For example, arXiv.org is a Physics-based repository.

BIBLIOGRAPHY

American Council of Learned Societies. "Our Cultural Commonwealth: The Report of the ACLS Commission on Cyberinfrastructure for the Humanities and Social Sciences (July 18, 2006)." http://www.acls.org/cyberinfrastructure/acls.ci.report.pdf.

Institute for Advanced Technology in the Humanities. "SDS Final Report." Charlottesville: University of Virginia, 2004. http://www3.iath.virginia.edu/sds/SDS_AR_2003.pdf.

Katz, Stanley N. "A Computer is Not a Typewriter, or Getting Right with Information Technology in the Humanities." http://www.wws.princeton.edu/snkatz/papers/uvatlk.html.

Lally, Ann M. and Joyce L. Ogburn. "Libraries and the Evolving Nature of Scholarship." In *Escholarship: A LITA Guide*, edited by Debra Shapiro, 25-41. Chicago: LITA Publications, 2005.

doi:10.1300/J167v08n02_13

Index

Acquisitions, 2-3
  in Central Asia
    problems facing U.S. libraries acquiring publications in, 36-37
    survey of U.S. libraries collecting in, 34-36
    U.S. library collecting strategies in, during glasnost' and perestroika, 33
    U.S. library collecting strategies in, during Soviet times, 32-33
    U.S. library collecting strategies in, since independence, 33-36
  in Greece, 2-3
  in Ukraine, 56-61
André Savine Collection, 4,96. *See also* *Russia Beyond Russia* Digital Library (RBR) resource discovery for, 106-107
Aneva, Sabina, 5
Anglo-American Cataloging Rules, 121
Architectural databases. *See* William Brumfield Russian Architecture Digital Collection
Art and Architecture Thesaurus (AAT) (Getty Museum), 121-122
Audio formats, 159

BASCL. *See* Central Library of the Bulgarian Academy of Sciences (BASCL)
Bashun, Olena, 3
Biggins, Michael, 4-5
Book-trading firms, Ukrainian, 59-60
Borodkin, Leonid, 3-4,6
Brown, Deborah, 51
Brumfield, William, 110-111,113,115

Brumfield architecture collection. *See* William Brumfield Russian Architecture Digital Collection
Bulgaria. *See* Central Library of the Bulgarian Academy of Sciences (BASCL)
Bushnell, John, 1-2

Cataloging Cultural Objects (Visual Resource Association), 111,121
Center for Educational Literature (Periodica), 59
Central Asia
  acquisitions in, 2-3
  collecting strategies in, during Soviet times, 32-33
  current collecting in, 35-36
  problems facing U.S. libraries acquiring publications in, 36-37
  survey of U.S. libraries collecting in, 34-36
  U.S. library collecting strategies in, during glasnost and perestroika, 33
  U.S. library collecting strategies in, during Soviet times, 32-33
  U.S. library collecting strategies in, since independence, 33-36
Central Library of the Bulgarian Academy of Sciences (BASCL), 5
  cataloging at, 138-149
  MARC21 at, 139,149
Collecting strategies. *See* Acquisitions
Commercial publishers, in Russia, 17-19
Consortium of Hellenic Studies Librarians (CoHSL), 51
Controlled vocabularies, 120-123

© 2007 by The Haworth Press, Inc. All rights reserved.

Copyrights, Stanley B. Winters collection and, 132-133
Core Module project, 4, 97-99. *See also* *Russia Beyond Russia* Digital Library (RBR)
   browsing by indexes of, 104
   data entry for, 103-104
   design of
      data content/structure for, 101
      data dictionaries for, 102
      record display interface, 102
      technical processing workflow, 103
      technical requirements for, 100-101
   kick-off meeting for, 99-100
   metadata structures for, 105-106
   overview of first phase of, 107
   project phases of, 99
Critical editions, 3
Czechoslovakia. *See also* Slovakia
   periodical press after Velvet Revolution in, 23-27
   periodical press before 1989 in, 22-23
Czech posters. *See* Zdenka and Stanley B. Winters collection

Daily press, in Slovakia, 24-25
Database design, objectives of, 116-119
Databases, access to, in Ukraine, 64-65
Digital scholarship, 6
   audio and, 159
   background of, 152-153
   barriers/constraints to management of, 153-155
   defined, 153
   enabling, librarian's role and, 156-161
   file formats and, 157-158
   funding, 157
   images and, 158-159
   librarians and, 155-156
   metadata standards for, 159-161
   preserving, 161
   providing access to, 161
   text files and, 158
   video and, 159
Digitization, 3-5
Dublin Core (DC), 160

East View Information Services (EVIS), 99-100
Electronic Library of the Faculty of History (Moscow State University), 4. *See also* *Russia Beyond Russia* Digital Library (RBR)
   contents of, 86-89
   Digital Sources section of, 89
   topic-oriented historical Internet resource (TOHIR) of, 90-92
Electronic resources
   created by Ukrainian institutions other than libraries, 57
   of Ukrainian libraries, 61-67
Encoded Archival Description (EAD), 131, 160
EVIS. *See* East View Information Services (EVIS)
Extensible Markup Language (XML), 160

Fesenko, Kirill, 99
File formats, 157-158
Formats
   audio, 159
   image, 158-159
   video, 159

Georgopoulou, Maria, 52
Gladney, Frank, 133
Glasnost', acquisition tactics during, 33
Greece
   acquisitions in, 2-3
   modern library collections of, 50-53
Greek collections, modern, 50-53

Index

Hswe, Patricia, 5

Iakovlev, Aleksandr, 19
Idea (Ukrainian subscription agency), 59-60
Image databases. *See* William Brumfield Russian Architecture Digital Collection
Image formats, 158-161
Imaging standards, 119-120

Kallista, Marie, 133
Kazakhstan, 40. *See also* Central Asia
Korolenko Kharkiv State Research Library (Ukraine), 63
Kraus, David H., 50
Kulla, Albert, 2
Kyrgyzstan, 41. *See also* Central Asia

Leich, Harold, 3
Lesage, Rhea Karabelas, 52
Levitt, Marcus, 3
Libkin, Olgert, 19
Librarians
  digital scholarship and, 155-156
  enabling digital scholarship and, 156-161
Libraries. *See* Ukraine
Library Forum of Ukraine (journal), 68
Library of the Verkhovna Rada (Supreme Council) of Ukraine, 66
Lindau, Rebecka, 51
Llona, Eileen, 6

MARC21 e-Club, 5
Metadata, 5-6
  encoding, 124
  standards for, 159-161
Metadata Encoding and Transmission Standard (METS), 105,111,160

Metadata Object Description Standard (MODS), 105,160
Middle Eurasian Books, 34
Modern Greek collections, 50-53
Modern Greek Studies Association (MGSA), 51
Monographs, 8
Monthly periodicals, in Slovakia, 25-26
Moscow State University. *See* Electronic Library of the Faculty of History (Moscow State University)

National Endowment for the Humanities (NEH), 157
National Library for Children (Ukraine), 63
National Parliamentary Library of Ukraine (NPLU), 62-63,66
National Scientific Medical Library (Ukraine), 63
Newspapers, in Slovakia, 24-25
Novikov, Nikolai, 76

Obligatory deposit, in Ukraine, 58
Oleksák, Peter, 2

Paganelis, George, 52
Pantelia, Maria, 52
Perestroika, acquisition tactics during, 33
Periodica (Center for Educational Literature), 59
Periodical press, before 1989, in Slovakia, 22-23
Perova, Nataliia, 19
Pilch, Janice, 133
Posters. *See* Zdenka and Stanley B. Winters collection
Private publishers, in Russia, 15-17
Publishing. *See also* Scholarly books
  in Kyrgyzstan, 41

in Russia, 1-2
in Slovakia, 2

Riley, Jacqueline, 51
Rondestvedt, Karen, 2-3
Ruble, Blair, 111
Russia. *See also* Textology, Russian
  commercial publishers in, 17-19
  private publishers in, 15-17
  publishing in, 1-2
  scholarly books in
    database for, 8-9
    funding for, 18-19
  publisher categories for, 9-14
Russia Beyond Russia Digital Library (RBR), 4. *See also* André Savine Collection; Core Module project; Electronic Library of the Faculty of History (Moscow State University)
  evolution of, 96-99
Russian history. *See* André Savine Collection; Electronic Library of the Faculty of History (Moscow State University); *Russia Beyond Russia* Digital Library (RBR); Textology, Russian; William Brumfield Russian Architecture Digital Collection
Russian State Archive of Ancient Acts (RGADA), 14

Savine, André, 96,97-99. *See also* André Savine Collection
Scholarly books
  defining, 8-9
  in Russia
    database for, 8-9
    funding for, 18-19
    private publishes for, 15-17

publisher categories for, 9-14
Scholarship. *See* Digital scholarship
Semikhenko, Oleg, 34
Serafínová, Danuša, 23
Slovak diaspora press, 26-27
Slovakia
  future of publishing in, 28
  introduction to, 22
  periodical press after Velvet Revolution
    daily press, 24-25
    monthly press, 25-26
    Slovak diaspora press, 26-27
    weekly press, 25
  periodical press before 1989 in, 22-23
  publishing in, 2
Slovak posters. *See* Zdenka and Stanley B. Winters collection
Subscription agencies, Ukrainian, 59
Sumarokov, Alexander, 75-78

Tajikistan, 38-39. *See also* Central Asia
Tasakopoulos Collection, 52
Text Encoding Initiative (TEI), 160
Text files, 158
Text library model, 4
Textology, Russian
  digital solutions and, 78-80
  eighteenth century texts and, 74-78
  from post-Soviet perspective, 72-74
Thesaurus Linguae Graecae, 52
Topic-oriented historical Internet resource (TOHIR) of Electronic Library, 4, 90-92
Tuchrello, Will, 34
Turkmenistan, 37. *See also* Central Asia

Ukraine
  access to databases in, 64-65
  acquisition methods in, 56-58
  acquisitions in, 2-3
  competitive bidding requirement in, 61
  electronic resources of libraries in, 61-67

library acquisition by purchase in, 58-61
library system of, 56
new professional journal for librarians in, 69
non-library electronic resources created in, 67
obligatory deposit in, 58
regional libraries in, 63-64
virtual reference services of libraries in, 68
websites of full-text resources in, 67
United States libraries
  collecting strategies of, for Central Asia
    during glasnost' and perestroika, 33
    since independence, 33-36
    during Soviet times, 32-33
  problems of, acquiring Central Asian publications, 36-42
Uzbekistan, 39-40. *See also* Central Asia

V. Sukhomlyns'kyi State Pedagogical Research Library, 66
V. Vernads'kyi National Library of Ukraine, 62,66
Valetov, Timur, 4,6
Van Duinen, Rita, 4,6,99
Velvet Revolution, Czechoslovakian periodical press after, 23-27
Video formats, 159
Virtual reference services, of Ukrainian libraries, 68
Vocabularies, controlled, 120-123

Web archives, 4
Weekly papers, in Slovakia, 25
William Brumfield Russian Architecture Digital Collection, 4-5
  controlled vocabularies and, 120-123
  database design objectives for, 116-119
  history of, 110-111
  imaging standards for, 119-120
  metadata encoding for, 124
  retrieval schemes and, 120-123
  significance of, 111-115
  storage, maintenance, and protection of, 124-126
Winters Stanley B., 128-129. *See also* Zdenka and Stanley B. Winters collection
Winters, Zdenka, 128-129. *See also* Zdenka and Stanley B. Winters collection
WorldCat, 4

XML (Extensible Markup Language), 160

Zachos, George, 51-52
Zapadov, V. A., 76
Zdenka and Stanley B. Winters collection, 5
  digitizing, 130-135
  highlights of, 129-130
  introduction to, 128-129
Zhivov, V. M., 75
Zilper, Nadia, 4,6,96,99